JGSB
10⁰⁰

Voodoo-EROS

Frontispiece—Three Tarusyots in Circumcision Custom and Author

Voodoo-EROS

ETHNOLOGICAL STUDIES IN THE SEX-LIFE
of the AFRICAN ABORIGINES

By **FELIX BRYK**
Translated from the German
By MAYNE F. SEXTON

UNITED BOOK GUILD
New York :: 1964

MANUFACTURED IN THE UNITED STATES OF AMERICA

CONTENTS

11

1. Watercarrier

INTRODUCTION

It is obviously impossible for one investigator to have studied through his own investigations all the sex questions among negro races with equal thoroughness. But the subject is of such importance, not only from the point of view of sexology, but also of ethnology and weltkultur, that we must be thankful to every one who brings us reliable information obtained through his own observation. The author of this work, Mr. Felix Byrk, has entirely succeeded in doing this in the following work. He who will be informed of the personal phenomena, and especially in

13

both sexes, will find excellent material here such as is not offered him anywhere else in a connected form. What we know of this subject is almost always to be found in single articles in periodicals, and, moreover, often described only by way of allusion. Here we have, as can be seen from the table of contents, and as the reader will recognize without difficulty, the subject described in connected book form. We are indeed indebted to the author for his descriptions and instruction. Whoever, in the future, would engage in the study of sex questions of the negro races, or do anything complete on it, will not be able to reach his goal without knowledge and study of this book. That various questions were discussed realistically could not be avoided. The stand that it is preferable to put such things in periodicals or archives, and not in independent books, is no longer tenable.

Nowadays the investigator has not the time to laboriously collect these things from numerous sources. It is a great advantage for him to have these questions treated connectedly in separate works.

DR. ALBERT MOLL.

2. Women in East-Central
Africa

AUTHOR'S FOREWORD

The reaction of the two sexes to each other is made steadfast by laws of nature, and which, like a thread of fire, runs through the whole animal kingdom, fixed for ever. The *ars amandi* may vary more or less according to the psychical or physical potency of the individual, according to his inexhaustible imagination, but the *modus amandi,* the relationship of the two loving beings to each other, remains constant through all times, all cultures, all races.

Only he who cannot comprehend the typical, the essential of a phenomenon in broad lines, will—led astray by a little unevenness, which his short-sightedness easily

15

turns into a heterogeneous occurrence—believe that he sees differences where the clear thinker, hampered by no prejudice, can find none.

Woman everywhere remains woman, and man remains man, independent of color, of skin and race, white or black, yellow or copper red: beyond the ugly and the beautiful, the old and the young, the good and the evil!

The material presented here, the gathering of which is due to my friend Professor John Almkyist of Stockholm, is for the purpose of revising the false conception we have about the differences of love in the different races. It will particularly show *that the negro woman by nature has desires and capabilities, emotions and feelings, in her sex life, that are no different from those of the white woman, in spite of the fact that she may not have reached the cultural level of the European woman.* And one will agree, in regard to erotic practices, with the idea expressed by Prof. Schweinfurth, that there are in Africa no other savages but those who have come from Europe.

In this work I have painstakingly sifted the material, often gathered with great labor, critically and objectively. Wherever it was possible, I have drawn from the very source of good and evil. The work has thereby received the value of something directly experienced, and is to that extent free of the dross which is part of the reports, more or less fictitious, based on hearsay. Only in exceptional cases have I relied upon reports, experiences and observations of others. As far as possible I avoided *direct questioning,* but rather, wherever I could, used circumlocutions, and put the question in an extensive form, in order that the natives grasp the point of the matter better and more plastically. It is quite difficult to obtain useful information from the blacks by direct questioning. For they like to lie, especially to the whites, as children often do, because they like children do not comprehend the moral demand of truthfulness. That is best noticed when honest old men, in relating folk tales, assure one, *bona fide,* that what they tell is true. Not only the picture that he draws, but also the picture he gives in words, takes on, with him, in the sense of Verworn, an ideoplastic form of expression; the moments that are thought, longed for, felt as forebodings, or made communal by a question, are to him experienced truths. A negro can talk abstractly as little as he can draw abstractly. He will constantly smuggle his individual experience into the picture of the typical.

For the investigation of our question I most preferably made use of the following method. If one of my guarantors—for example, a black woman—betrayed a valuable detail that was unknown to me by an *inadvertently spoken* word or an involuntary manifestation of emotion, I asked the person about it without arousing suspicion, and then tested the information obtained in the same manner with other people of the same tribe, both sexes, if possible. Or I did not ask about it at all, but manifested that emotion before the blacks who belonged to the same tribe as my guarantor, *e. g.,* the sulking of coyness of the black wife, in order to see the effect which my mimic play had upon the faces of my spectators. If I noticed that the blacks were agreeably surprised in wonder at my knowledge, then I knew that I was on the right track, for the recognition of a depicted occurrence calls forth a feeling of joy in every one. Findings that were fragmentary or doubtful were tested by repeated observations. When I could get no sure result, I give the facts with reservation.

While it is really not very difficult to penetrate into the sex life of the black woman, because she does not conceal her love-emotions as much as the white woman does, and —without being in any way obscene—answers questions on sex, it is not so easy to obtain information from the woman (nor from the man) on sex rites. It is as if she were bound by a religious vow—especially the Nandi— to be silent on these questions. For example, it was only through mere chance that I succeeded in learning something about circumcision from a Nandi woman with whom I was very intimate; and it was a stroke of good fortune that another woman as the same time (!)—without having the least idea of the report made to me by the above mentioned Nandi—told my white neighbor entirely corresponding details. Later she could not be brought to say more on this question, and I could see quite plainly that she suffered because she had betrayed to me, a white man, the secret of her tribe. I had to give the Nandi warrior who told me about his circumcision a relatively high remuneration of five shillings; at the same time I had to assure him that I would not betray a word of it to a Nandi; otherwise he would be lost. I had him tell me the whole story twice—the second time after an interval of ten days—both reports corresponded. I made use of them for my investigations later by casually asking questions of negroes at their rites of circumcision, the answers confirmed my earlier findings or supplemented them with small details.

My guarantors consisted of black laborers, medicine men, Ashkaris, servants, girls, peasants and their wives, and naturally, for certain questions, representatives of the negro youth.

I hope that, through my love for the subject, I have not gone to the other extreme and exchanged the common contempt for the black for a sentimental overestimation of the negro. It was also far from my purpose to spice the taste of certain readers with obscene stories and pictures. My position to the question under consideration is that of a research worker to a biological phenomenon that is being investigated: to penetrate deeper into its nature by elucidation and investigation of all its phases. The comprehensive literature pertaining to the subject was purposely not taken into consideration in order not to influence what has been presented here by observations and statements of my predecessors.

Collected material is fragmentary. I am entirely conscious of this. It is only a matter of a sample taken offhand, for a life span would hardly be sufficient for an exhaustive treatment of the subject, which I have only outlined.

Every negro tribe has its own peculiarities, often differing materially from the erotic customs, usages and habits of neighboring tribes. In the time of the two years that I spent here in Equatorial Africa, north of Victoria Nyanza, I had the opportunity to investigate the sex life of only the few tribes with whom chance brought me in contact. Of the Bantu tribes: the Bagishu,[1] Baganda,[2] Budama,[3] Banioro,[4] Kitosh,[5] Kikuyu, Maragoli[5] Kavirondo,[5] Suaheli;[6] of the Semi-hamites: the Nandi,[7] Wandorobbo,[8] Tiriki,[9] Aldai,[9] Sebeyi,[10] Elkoyni,[10] Suk.[11] At every description of a fact, the tribe to which it has reference is always put in parentheses, because all the hundreds of tribes and races that populate Africa cannot simply be designated by the single collective noun "negro." Facts given do not have to be taken to refer only to the tribe mentioned; they may just as well be proved to apply to other tribes, but I have not discovered it. A fact is consequently always to be received with this reservation.

Mount Elgon, 2350 meters high, in the year 1925.

---

[1] Northern Elongo territory near Mbale.
[2] The inhabitants of Uganda proper.
[3] Southwest of Mt. Elgon near Tororo.
[4] West of Uganda (Toro).
[5] In the Kavidondo basin, northwest of Victoria Nyanza.
[6] The inhabitants of the coast near Mombassa.
[7] Southwest of Mt. Elgon on the Nandi plateau near Kapsabet.
[8] In the Mau Mountains near Njoro.
[9] Northwest of Port Florence near Kaimosi.
[10] Territory northwest of Mt. Elgon.
[11] North of Mt. Elgon.

3. Native in Ceremonial
Dress

CLOTHING

The dress of negroes is much more uniform than one would at first think. I have often experienced difficulty in distinguishing men from women at a distance by their clothes.

The negro of today generally wears his piece of cloth or his sleeping cover—for the customary negro dress is in reality nothing more—deftly thrown over his shoulder in fine folds, draped like a toga, and fastened by a knot,

21

•

a piece of string or a safety pin. The woman as a rule wraps herself in white cotton cloth, with colored stripes only above and below, in such a manner that the upper part of her shoulders, her head, neck and arms, are exposed to the top of her breasts, while the upper corner of the dress is tucked into the cloth under one shoulder. As in the Italian Quattrocentists, the straight, vertical appearance of the torso, because of the very long garment, sets

4. Nandi-Boyot   5. Nandi Old Man

off in fine contrast the nude upper part of the body. A piece of material like sack-cloth, often with ornamental coloring serves as a sash to hold the garment fast about the loins. Under this simple dress, which gives the body a slender appearance, there is often found (Baganda) an

22

apron-like undergarment, shorter above, which envelopes the body in the same way as the outer garment; this is also held fast by a sash. Among the poorer Bagishu there is often only the single outer garment: in a strong wind, if both ends of the cloak open below, the pubic region becomes visible. If a girl or woman wishes to expose her breasts, as, for example, while working or dancing, she simply loosens the cloth under her shoulder, lets it fall

6. Kitosh Woman in
Usual Dress

down to the sash, and tucks the loose, free upper part of the cotton material, together with both ends, behind her hips, and the womanly charm of the breasts, the abdomen and the back appear in all their beauty as in an antique torso, while the garment has in this simple manner become a skirt. Seam and buttons are unknown to this negro dress.

23

This is how the usual dress of the *bibi** looks today, if it has not yet been contaminated by the tasteless European fashion. Among well-to-do women (Baganda), especially among prostitutes, the cotton dress is replaced

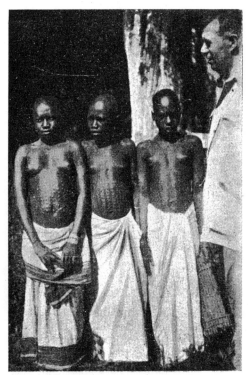

7. Three Cannibal Women
and the Author

---

* Bibi is the general term for a woman (Kisuaheli).

Some time ago, German wool were put on the market from Mombassa, distinguished by a special inscription printed on them: *unkinipendo—ntakunipenda* (I love him—who loves me). Sometimes this statement was on the breast, sometimes on the buttocks—according to the cut; in both cases it is supposed to have had a very coquettish and inviting effect.

24

by one of silk, which is gaily colored, full of folds, trails behind, and often reaches down to the ankles and knuckles. This, like the long shirt (*kansu*) of the men and the inseparable parasol of coquettish loose women, is to be traced to the influence of the Arab or Arabized population of the coast.

Footwear is not very important. Wherever it is found in the form of sandals made of buff or zebra-leather it is

8. Two Prostitutes

9. Osotya

exclusively the privilege of the men. It functions as a means of transportation, like snow shoes, helping the black traveller over mud and thorny underbrush, and not as an article of clothing. When not worn they are carried suspended from the staff which the negro invariably carries. In Uganda I obtained a very beautiful pair of slippers, in the form of a boat, painted red, white and blue-black on the inside, made of thick buff, but which were not, as is usual, fastened about the foot with laces, but were held fast around the great toe and heel by means of a ready-made noose of an otter fur. The grace and beauty of these sandals attest to the fact that they are worn only by the feminine sex. Wooden slippers, with heels, in front

10. Nandi Woman Working

and behind, and which are held fast by a projecting button between the large and second toe, allow the finer, cleaner Uganda population, both men and women, to wade through the mud outside the hut, during the rainy season, as if on stilts. Indoors they are put aside.

It is not difficult to make the usual clothing of women as described from animal skins, as it is the case among the Semi-hamitic shepherd peoples (Nandi, Sebeyi, Suk, Elkoyni). There the entire body covering consists of two leather aprons, made of cow-hide. The upper apron, the larger and longer one, is held together over one shoulder by narrow laces, as in the already described masculine

11. Warrior in Parade
Dress

toga. Thus the arm, and often the breast on the opposite side remains exposed. This apron may also be fastened around the neck. The mantle, hanging thus loosely, readily allows the breast to peep out, while the under apron, which is fastened around the waist on a side, exposes the slender legs of its wearer to view as the ends rise and fall in walking, much as was the fashion in certain styles during the *Empire,* and as it was at the beginning of this century in the case of the slashed skirt. Small girls and shepherd boys do not wear the under apron at all and the pubic region is exposed by every move, which, as also the buttocks, is only in exceptional cases covered before and behind by square pieces of cloth attached to a sash around the hips. In this leather garment the breasts, abdomen and back may be exposed as desired, in a manner similar to that in the usual dress, by allowing the upper part to fall down to the girdle.

Europeanized Nandi women and girls always wear over their short-sleeved, striped cotton dresses, which is worn rather tight around the body, a large colored cotton shawl. This covering of the breasts, which stand out under the dress, is mainly for the purpose of hiding them from the eyes, or more correctly, the evil eye of jealous and envious women, as a typical representative of the Nandi tribe quite solemnly assured me. All these new styles come from the coast: from the Suahelis, who seem to be the leaders here not only in customs and diffusion of their language, but also in venereal diseases and the refining of erotic art. But may it here be emphasized again that the clothing of men and women was originally not differentiated according to the Islamitic and European customs.

This primitive mode of dress was preceded by a condition of almost complete lack of clothing, if not nakedness, as we still find it today among the Kavirondo women on the northeast shore of Victoria Nyanza. The feminine sex usually wears in front a small apron of fibres on a girdle of inner bark, by which the *mons veneris* is barely covered; behind hangs a tail of fibres, which lies close in the anal fissure, and which has more the signification of an amulet than of an ornament. Except for this, the body is entirely naked. Among the Budama this nudity is much more charming. The only piece of clothing (*ndagala*) among the girls and women consists of a little skirt about seven or eight inches long of feathered banana-leaf fibres, which, hanging, low around the hips, from an inner girdle of bark, hardly reach the pubic region, which often becomes visible in walking. The green of this extremely short ballet skirt lends their black wearers a special charm. The boys there go about entirely nude, and the men who have not yet been influenced by missionaries or other bearers of foreign culture, wear only two little aprons on a girdle in front and behind, barely large enough to cover anus and membrum.

When one considers that in Uganda, which has been strongly influenced by Christianity and Islam, nudity has been almost entirely done away with, and that in spite of the tropic heat, which constantly prevails there, has given place to warm heavy clothing, long woolen stockings and heavy shoes, but that in the cooler, even cold regions north of Mt. Elgon, the sparse clothing has maintained itself among the heathen tribes, one cannot help concluding, that clothing has not been introduced as a protection against cold, but that it is rather dictated by purely esthetic reasons, or forced upon the negro by missionaries of various religious sects to give him the sense of shame at the uncovering of those parts of the body that are erotically active, a feeling originally entirely strange to him.

Nothing impresses the negro more than European clothing. Give a *Shenzi** a threadbare, heelless stocking,

---

* Man of the forest; usual contemptuous expression for a "wild man."

and he will joyfully thank you for it, and go about in it while his other foot remains bare.

The stocking on the foot of the naked negro-boy in hot Equatorial Africa on the one hand, and the delicately spun silk stockings on the legs of the European woman, in the severest winter frost, on the other, are determined by the same desire for erotic charm and love of admiration.

12. African Beauties

13. Elkoyni Girls

Ornament

Among the negroes, especially among the Massaioid shepherd peoples, the mark of sex, which has been hidden by the sameness of the clothing, is indirectly made evident again by ornament which cancel the levelling of the sexes. According to their ornament, man and woman, girl and boy, can easily be distinguished, even at a distance.

The head ornament of the girls, consisting of white and colored glass bead strings, separates the closely trimmed or shaved head from the forehead at the temples (Sebeyi, Elkoyni, Nandi); a feather is often stuck in the middle of the forehead. These strings are pushed down from the

14. Chief and His Family

head to the neck at work, or more correctly, before completely "dressing"; in this case a few green blades of grass wound around the forehead nicely replaces the string of beads. Sometimes the string is pushed down under the nose, which looks pert and from a distance looks like white moustache. This string of beads becomes a head-dress like a diadem, if, instead of beads, a row of cowrie-shells sewed on the leather in the midst of which is set a socket of tin into which a grey-brown ostrich feather is boldly stuck,

32

it then gives the wearer of this ornament a fascinating appearance. A considerably more modest impression is made by a trouser-button or a cowrie-shell, often worn by men on a string around the forehead, which, however, is always covered by a leather cap (Bagishu). The cap is a good mark for distinguishing between man and woman,

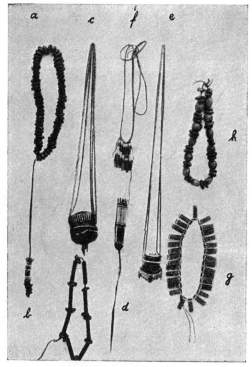

15. Ornaments of the Nandi

since it belongs exclusively to male ornamentation. It is made of the stomach of a cow and is usually oiled with fat and red earth; it lies close to the skull like an aviator's cap (Nandi, Suk). The old men wear a similar one, of shining, black cowhide, held fast by a closely-lying hat-guard; the beads sewed on, with the very short chain hanging down in front, is meant to take the place of the colored beads worn by the younger men around the head on their caps. Lately, two-pointed caps of white cotton, red or grey stocking-like material has been put on the market by the Indians. The men hide their pig-tails or their false manes under it (Nandi).

16. Medicine Man

Ornament for the forehead is to be found only in girls or young women. I have come across it only among the

Nandi and the Lumbwa, where it belongs more to pomp than to everyday dress. It is supposed to take the place of a kind of veil and consists of strings of beads connected vertically by colored beads and little copper chains, and reaches from the forehead to the eyebrows (*Kilisik*). *Songonyet* is another forehead ornament of the Nandi, worn only on the occasion of the death of a brother or

17. Nandi with Stone
Ear-Block

sister, serving as an amulet. Girls tie it onto their tufts of hair, isolated in front, the rest of the head being shaved. It consists of a round piece of leather with concentric strings of beads set around a button, from which short chains hang over the upper half of the forehead. Over the circle of beads a cowrie-shell is set. The married woman then wears it on a chain around her neck as an ornament for her breasts. We must mention yet the *tilec* of the circumcised: a small tassel made of pieces of leather and white beads, but which enjoys no special popularity (Nandi).

The heavy iron, very wide neck-rings (the *merenget* of the Nandi) are more typical of the feminine sex than of the masculine. Little children who can hardly walk

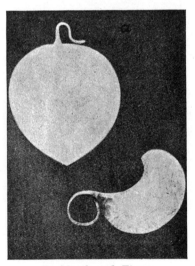

18. Mouth and Finger
Ornaments

are already supplied with it, in order, even at this early age to mark the difference of the sexes (Sebeyi, Nandi, Tiriki). Black glossy beads strung together, with or without bamboo sticks between them, are also worn around the neck by young girls until puberty (*lapuonic*). While similarly to the *songonyet* mentioned above, the *sepetaic* is venerated as an amulet by the boys and girls of those families in which all the older brothers and sisters have died. It consists of small, perforated yellow-brown pieces of the neck of a calabash through which a leather string has been drawn. Between every piece, perforated English

19. Nandi Woman

copper coins, the copper money of the negro, is inserted. This they have learned through watching their mothers, who love to wear all kinds of pendants from their necks, especially African copper money. Broad iron plates strung

37

together are often supposed to give the impression of coins; originally, no doubt, representing capital (Nandi, Elkoyni). The men of the Kikuyu wear very tightly fitting bands around their necks, which are usually made of leather thongs set with white and blue glass beads, which has a very coquettish effect, and together with the splendid girdle, embroidered with beads, and the tender, silver-

20. Application of the
Segenge

white tin earrings, gives the masculine sex an expression that is, according to European ideas, feminine, and sometimes even perverse. The vain Suk men content themselves with deep blue, coarse strings of beads, while the proud Nandi now and then wears a chain about his neck which consists of loose pieces of leather, onto each of which three copper wire spirals and a few beads have been sewed. Usually, however, copper and iron chains are the emblem of a man, from which often hangs a snuff-box artistically carved out of ox horn (the *kivraut* of the Nandi), a calabash (Nandi), or wood (Kamba), or one piece of horn (Suk, Wandorobbo); lately all this is being superceded by a brass cartridge-case for the same purpose. It also has some esthetic signification in the dance, the dangling of the box when the dancer bounds into the air being considered to have something very masculinely beautiful about it, and the phallo-symbolic signification of which is easily seen. May it be emphasized that the ring and chain about the neck serve the purpose of receiving all kinds of amulets, such as pieces of wood (Elkoyni, Nandi) turtle scales (Bagishu), turtle necks (Suk), pieces of leather of the medicine-men, leopard teeth or baubles of sheet-iron (Tiriki).

The ornamentation of the ear is quite striking. For its reception, from earliest youth, in both sexes, the margin of the external ear is perforated, and at first little sticks of bamboo or other match-like pieces of wood are inserted to keep the hole open, later all kinds of glass bead rings, cowrie-shells, safety pins (very popular), and little chains (Nandi). Among the Suk women the ear is very much broadened by the insertion of brass rings along the margin of the perforated ear. I have observed something similar among the Geluo. It is the custom among the Kikuyu women to set a great many large wire rings, five inches in diameter, along the edge of the ear in a very decorative manner, so that from a distance one is reminded of the once popular head-dress of shells, which the rings

very much resemble. But the real ear ornament hangs,
or rather is set, in the unusually extended hole of the
pierced lobe of the ear, which, among the Nandi, is made
with the arrow (*longnet*) used for letting the blood of
cows, and is so widened by the insertion of tufts of leaves,
pegs of wood, and cigarette-boxes, that its thin lower edge
hangs down loosely like an india rubber band. The Nandi

21. Kyepta with
Ear-Blocks

22. Nandi Married Woman

men stretch the skin of the ear by means of heavy pendants, artistically made of tin or copper wire, or smooth,
silver-loking tin plates, bi-angular, spade-shaped or polished fluted blocks of soap-stone, carved into the form of a
barrel. Boys and girls must be content with more or less

40

thick pegs of wood,* (Nandi, Lumbwa), like rolling pins, which are sometimes nicely polished. The Kikuyu have gone a step further: they use large iron rings, like napkin rings, for the distension of the hole of the ear. The married Nandi women succeed better in distending this loosely hanging, cartilage-free skin of the lobe of the ear by inserting into each of the holes a leather bow (*Amuita*).

However hideous at first the pendent skin of the ear may seem to the unaccustomed eye, the ear as a whole, after a time, with all its weights, pegs and beads, appears grotesquely beautiful. Without ornament, however, this drooping somatic embellishment looks highly unpleasant, of which the owners seem to be fully conscious, since in this case they wind the loose lower skin over the top margin of the ear, whereupon the ear now, though still deformed, does not look morbidly mutilated, as it does with the folds of brown skin hanging down. Many a pretty Nandi wench, who, under the influence and spell of European fashion, has cast away her beautiful national costume for ever, deplores nothing more than the presence of these ugly strands of skin, which, out of all connection with the adornment she now wears for her ears, has become an object of derision of the neighboring peoples, especially the Baganda. For the Baganda have done away with all artificial somatic embellishments, thanks to the intervention of King Daudi, who has been strongly influenced by Christianity. Neither the smashing of the lower incisors, universally practiced by other tribes on young children, nor the perforation of the ear, nor the decorating of the

---

* I have taken a peg from the ear of a Nandi that was nine inches long, had a circumference of seven inches and weighed nearly a pound.

body with scars is allowed in Uganda. Whoever resists is liable to severe penalties, such as the confiscation of his cattle; but as a consequence the negro in Uganda has sunk to the level of a neatly dressed European dandy, and for all that he is not indifferent to decorations and ornament.

Like the ear, the under lip has also developed into a bearer of ornament: it is perforated and all kinds of objects are inserted into it. A typical lip ornament for the women of the Kovirondo are stoppers of bevelled, milk-white, vulcanic glass, but a piece of wood,* of a similar form, may serve the same purpose. Imported nails, screws (Sebeyi), a piece of iron wire (Suk), are also used; short cork-shaped objects that are thicker at one end that they might not slip through the hole in the lip. By pressure of the tongue the stopper, raised above the lip, is removed, which sometimes happens while laughing. In men I have seen this ornament only among the Semi-hamitic Suk, who also possess a very remarkable decoration for the mouth. It consists of a large plate, beaten as thin as paper from a piece of tin wire which ends in a hook that is anchored in the central cartilage of the nose† and completely covers the mouth and even the stopper in the lip. It is amusing to see how this bracteate-like ornament moves back and forth while speaking or eating.

The upper and forearm is adorned in a most striking and peculiar manner, extreme cases being shown by the

---

* The assertion that only young coquettish women wore stone stoppers, and the old women wooden ones is not correct; I repeatedly saw old women wearing them made of stone.

† Neither ornament of the nose, nor that of the upper lip is found among the tribes I studied, but the former is widespread on the coast.

Massaioid Nandi women. The greater part of the upper
arm down to the knuckle of the elbow, and the fore-arm
down almost as far as the wrist is encased, as in a cuff, by
armor formed by closely wound iron or brass wire
(*segenge*) in the form of a spiral. This extreme development of ornament, which strikes the eye even from a distance, is the most reliable ornamental sign of the woman.
The galvanized iron glistens like silver and the brass like

23. Nandi Warrior with
Bracelet

gold. When one sees a Nandi woman in these adornments
for the first time, which, moreover, are also worn on the
calf of the leg, he is inclined to believe at first that some

solemn occasion or unusual event is the cause of her wearing those heavy, massive rings. But on closer observation he readily sees how inseparable from the body this uncomfortable ornamentation is. She is seen in it every day, with the cattle, in the field, in the hut. With this ornamentation on her she cooks, chops her wood, pastures, milks, and cultivates her land. Indeed, she does not put aside this cold, cumbersome armor when she sleeps, sacrificing every comfort. Even if she should wish to, she could not remove it. Once applied, it clings to her soft body for life. It can be gotten rid of only if it is destroyed by unwinding, which light-minded wenches, who are ashamed of their original national costume, are induced

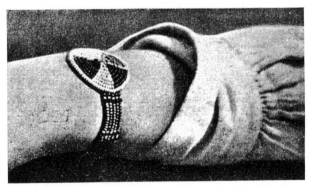

24. Nandi Bead Bracelet

to do. The exposed skin, which has been severely attacked over a long period of time by verdigris or other poisons given off by the metal, and the constant pressure of the tightly drawn rings, now becomes covered with ugly, permanent scars, as if by welts. Like all womenly ornamentation, these *segenge,* which on the arm are called

44

karnet, on the leg *tabakwe,* are also the work of feminine domestic industry. There are women who specialize in the application of these bracelets, and it is really marvellous to see how skillfully they can wind these serpentine rings, without any instrument, around the arm and leg of their clients, from one piece of iron wire about five yards long, imported from England. Since these women usually also practice the art of circumcision, it is comprehensible, that after circumcision, likely as not, some woman gives them business to increase her ornament or exchange her iron rings for the more highly prized brass ones. In small girls such *segenge* are much more unassuming, that is, shorter; they are sometimes absent altogether. But a Nandi woman without that armor is unthinkable. Men too, especially old men, sometimes wear *segenge,* but short ones, only around the region of the wrist, usually made of fine copper wire which is closely wound on top of the usual iron spirals, so that the iron is completely covered by it. They are about two inches wide (Nandi, Elkoyni, Sebeyi).

The bracelet for the upper arm, around the armpit, is very popular. It fits so tightly, that the pressure of it, especially in women, causes a marked swelling of the upper arm. In women it is made of strings of beads and is worn on both arms (*sanoyek*). The men wear this ornament only on the upper arm; it is forged mostly of iron, and usually goes only once around the biceps (*samoyot*). How tightly it fits can be seen from the fact that one which an elderly Nandi wore measured only about three inches in diameter. A string of beads made out of fragments of ostrich eggs that have been cut round (*kelekik*)

45

is used by both men and women for therapeutic purposes, especially for rheumatism (Nandi). Very simple and elegant is a bracelet for the upper arm that is made of two crescent-shaped tusks of the warthog, which, perforated on both sides, are connected by two leather bands.

That the wrist region furnishes opportunity for wearing all kinds of bracelets of iron (Tiriki, Bagishu), strings of beads (Nandi), leather thongs (Bagishu) need not be emphasized when one remembers how widespread this ornament is even among ourselves. But I mention in particular the massive, heavy, half-open iron rings of the Sebeyi and Bagishu women, the black serpentine rings of the hair from the tail of the giraffe, decorated with a few tiny cowrie-shells (Bagishu women), and the very elegant leather bracelets, heavy set with bright colored beads, which in the middle have a concentric coil of glass beads —looking somewhat like our watch bands (Lumbwa, Nandi, Kikuyu).

The finger ring is a hand ornament that is widespread everywhere. Among the negroes the thumb especially seems to have developed into the ring-finger: it is encircled by an iron spiral about one-half inch wide (men of the Elkoyni, Sebeyi, etc.). I need not dwell over the bizarre rings that are imported from Europe and India, an ornament that is exceedingly popular with the young and old. But I note the grotesque hide-ring of the shepherd peoples, which is worn only by men on the middle finger. It consists of a narrow pierced strip of goat or cow hide and is probably more of an amulet than an ornament proper. It is worn only on the special occasion, several days after the slaughtering of of a goat or cow, and then only when the black soothsayer has read from the stomach of the slaughtered animal that it is healthy, and can conclude from that the well being of his friends; then it is put away, sometimes added by his wife to the many pendant trinkets hanging from her neck-band. The calf, when slaughtered, must have been not older than one day; it then has that silky gloss which older ones have not. I once saw a village sultan of the Nandi with three such hide-rings (*tamoket*) on one finger; he presented me with one of them. The quite peculiar *akol* of the Suk, more a murderous weapon than a ring, will be discussed in the treatment of head-dress.

The two plate-shaped spirals (*taok*) of the Nandi woman, wound of brass wire, is one of the most beautiful and original, yet simplest, of ornaments created by women's fantasy. They are worn only by the married woman, being put on directly after the promotion of the circumcised into the official status of bride. They are worn on a short iron chain or narrow leather strap in such a manner as to reach down to the breasts without covering them. The weight of this dangling breast ornament in time somewhat flattens the breasts. A young widow must remove these brass plates. But if a married woman shows herself without the *taok*, the man's sense of decency seems to be injured by this negligee. A Nandi warrior gave me a stick and asked me to beat his wife who had appeared outside the hut without her breast ornament. Soon afterwards, however, she did appear with her *taok*, thereby enhancing the beauty of her bosom. If a woman goes about without a *taok*, her husband thinks she is wishing for his death, for a woman without a *taok*, as has been mentioned, is the sign that she is a widow. Genetically these breast plates may be derived from the quite similar, hanging ear ornament of the Massai women. They have simply slipped down from the ears to the breasts. Perhaps that is the reason why the *taok* is tied, by means of a leather strip, to the *muita,* which ends in a glass bead as large as a gooseberry.

The girdle of four rows of cowrie-shells of the Sebeyi women (also of the Nandi bride) is half ornament, half article of clothing. On the one hand, it plays the same part as the hip sash of the usual dress—that of holding together the leather garment—and on the other hand, the cowrie-shells sewed onto this leather girdle, which is about three inches wide, serve no other purpose than that of ornamentation. The Kikuyu-Morans also wear a girdle on which are sewed glass beads, and little copper chains, which reminds one of ancient Egyptian beadwork; its purpose is likewise purely ornamental. Otherwise I know only of girdles, weapon belts for swords, to which at times tufts of hair from a lion's mane are attached as amulets (Nandi), or a nut-like fruit serving as a medicine. Actual hip ornamentation is usually hidden from the eye of the observer, since it is worn covered by the dress. It consists in a single or double string of beads (*tundu*), which is sometimes worn tight (Nandi), and sometimes so loose that it dangles down to the pubic region; this, as a Massai woman assured me, serves to intensify the *libido sexualis* during the act. The man rolls this love-girdle up and down on the abdomen of the woman with the palm of his hand, which is supposed to cause a pleasant erotic sensation in him and the woman. Men also like to wear such

48

sashes, which among the Nandi often becomes an actual girdle of beads; among the Suk it often consists of small iron chains. In lieu of a *tundu,* a loose sash may also form this hip and loin ornament. Quite original is the *kisansa* of the Budama an Mnioro girls—an oval strip of wood, covered with checkered bast braiding, and looking like a snake-skin, which is pulled up over the leg and set aside at bed time. It measures about eight inches inside and ten outside.

The hip sash of little girls (Elkoyni) is often hung with any number of meaningless pendants. One need simply go one step further and imagine a systematic attachment of homogeneous pieces of ornamentation to the loin sash, and one has the *osyek,* the trim fringe apron of the Nandi girls. Beads or strings of pea-like fruit hang alternately with narrow strips of leather from a slender strap set with a row of cowrie-shells; they are set so close together that they form what is almost an apron. Only uncircumcised girls (*kyepta*) wear this elegant ornament, which is hidden under their leather or cotton mantles when they do not go about altogether naked.

The buttock ornamentation of the Kawirondo women has already been mentioned. Another decoration for the covering of this part is the *goysit* of the Nandi-*morans* which consists of a shield-shaped piece of calf-skin, usually white and bent over on top.

I do not know of any ornamentation of the thigh.

The ornamentation of the shank, *tabakwe,* of the Nandi girls and women, which is to be considered ornamentation of the calf has already been mentioned in the discus-

sion of the *segenge*. Otherwise only the ankle is ornamented, by means of an ordinary string, a band of glass
beads (Kikuyu men), rings of copper wire wound together like a spiral spring or with long shaggy pieces of
ape or goat skin decorated with beads (Nandi men). The
massive, thick, but loose rings of iron, of which the women
of the Sebeyi and Elkoyni wear two, look like fetters on
the feet of prisoners, and, beating together during walking, give out a clashing, loudly ringing metallic sound. I
cannot help thinking of the idea that once suggested itself
to me, that this ringing serves a purpose similar to that
of cow bells, to indicate to the husband the whereabouts
or the presence of his rambling wife from a distance. Such
a woman cannot easily enter into a rendezvous with another man without being heard by others; unless she shove
both rings up to her calves and insert green leaves between
the calf and the ring to keep them from sliding down
again. I sometimes noticed in travelling women who thus
prevented being caught in the underbrush of the jungle.
Perhaps this foot ornament was originally a calf ring, and
to be considered as having slipped down from the calf to
the foot.

I could determine still another *musical foot ornament*
among the men (Nandi, Elkoyni, Kawirondo). It consists of one to ten little iron bells bound tightly around
the ankle on a strip of leather. In walking they emit a
pleasant, gently ringing sound which may betray the dangerous hunter to the wild beasts, or they announce to the
women the approach of their lover, or their lord and
master.

50

Iron rings around the toes, especially the big toe, are seldom worn (Nandi). I have been told that they are meant to be a protection against thorns.

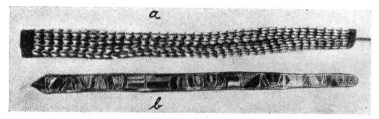

25. Girdles

26. Nandi Hair-Dress

HAIR-DRESS

The fundamental nature of ornament is simply that of calling forth esthetic effect by means of foreign, usually anorganic objects on the human body, as is produced in the animal kingdom by means of somatic embellishments. Accordingly, one sees in ornament a completion, an intensification, even a surrogate for the somatic sexual ornamentation that is not very striking in man. But besides this decoration the human being has found a means of producing ornamentation directly from his body, by special treatment of his hair and skin.

In general the hair of the head is worn cut close or

entirely shaved so that one cannot distinguish the two sexes by the hair alone. All kinds of flutes (*kinansa* of the Suaheli) through the frizzed, much matted wooly hair are very popular, or quite fantastic islands of hair on the

27. Warrior with Pig-Tail

otherwise completely shaved head, which sometimes are worn as a sign of mourning (Bagishu) over the loss of their children, or, by children, as a mark of magic, when their older brothers and sisters have died. The warriors of certain shepherd peoples (Nandi, Suk, Kikuyu, Massai) wear their hair long to increase their manliness. The system of short braids, introduced from the coast by the

53

Suahelis, is very popular, especially among the Europeanized Nandi prostitutes, consists of the one-half inch long woolly hair being separated into innumerable, short, wormlike parallel plaits; in this way many lines appear on the scalp, running from front to back. It is impossible for a negress to do all this by herself; so she turns to an experienced hair dresser who receives as fee from a half to a whole shilling. The aforementioned head-dress of the men requires no little patience, since it is in great part made of false *hair*. Black or blue-black yarn from an unravelled sweater or some piece of cotton goods is tied to each individual hair by means of fine threads, so that finally there is a mane, reaching down to the shoulders, while in front a short tuft of hair, cut obliquely, runs down to the forehead, and one on each side to the temples (Nandi). Like this mane, the pig-tail of the Nandi-*morans,* which is likewise made of unravelled yarn, requires lengthy treatment by a man hair-dresser, who is always found among his friends working gratuitously. When the pig-tail has been braided together, the story is by no means finished. It is wound in a bandage of white cotton like a mummy until it looks like a stiff peg. On top of that is wound a narrow strip of goat's leather, which a girl set thickly with glass beads, so that finally the pig-tail completely disappears beneath a fine bead trimming. As has been mentioned, the mane and pig-tail are usually hidden under a cap, and exposed only at the dance.

Many Semi-hamitics rub in their long hair with loam and tallow so that it receives a set consistency that often becomes crustaceous (Suk and the medicine men of the Nandi). That the bearer of such a painstakingly acquired

head-dress, in which all sorts of small objects are im-
bedded, will try to keep his hair in order as long as possible, is easily comprehensible, especially when it is so difficult to *recomb*. For this purpose the Suks have invented
a special piece of furniture that allows them to sleep with-

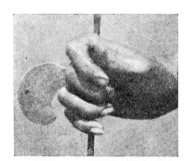

28. Akol Finger Ring

out spoiling their *wigs*. This is a small, finely polished stool
(*natsher*), the seat of which is slightly concave to allow
the temple or neck of the sleeper to rest comfortably on
it while the head-dress hangs outside. It is a hair protector
and a pillow at the same time. These cushions are made
very elegant and neat, and there is no Suk who does not
have such a sleeping stool on his travels, on which he can
also sit down. Among the Sebeyi, who have no very striking hair-dress, this *natsher* has become larger and clum-
sier; it serves them as a support while squatting.

An iron chain one yard long that ends in a little piece

of downy ass-skin hangs down from the head dress of every Suk as if to take the place of a pig-tail; in addition, an ostrich feather, boldly stuck in front, is worn at times.

Combing of the kinky hair is also found among certain negro tribes (Kitosh, Kavirondo, less often Nandi). Wooden, primitive combs are used, which are often worn by the men in their hair; sometimes a wooden hair-pin is used for this purpose (Nandi). Scissors are unknown to the negro. He cuts and shaves his hair by means of a knife or piece of glass; recently with razors, even with Gillette blades. The *akol*, the razor of the Suk, is quite original. This is an iron ring that is worn on the middle finger and spreads out into a sharp blade 3 inches long and about two inches wide. If one sees a Suk with such a catch on his finger, one thinks at first that it is simply some grotesque ring, somewhat in the style of his bracteate-like lip plate; but if one notices the sharp blade, which serves another purpose than simply shaving, one changes his hypothesis and recognizes in the *akol* a weapon murderous when the occasion demands.

One can often surprise negro men and women in front of their huts at their favorite occupation: that of shaving the head (Kitosh, Bagishu, Baganda). Here too the Nandi have set strict barriers between men and women: among them as a rule men shave reciprocally and the women by themselves. The head is usually shaved smooth so that the craniums of both sexes shine like a pate; but among many tribes it is a popular custom to shave away the periphery of the woolly skull, so that the hair proper (*piur* of the Nandi) now sharply bounded, has the appearance of a fine woollen bonnet, giving the women especially an elegant aspect. Now if this woollen bonnet is allowed to grow to a length of about two inches, as the fair sex of the Suk does, the absence of combing produces the hair of a Fury, which has anything but an esthetic affect upon us. If the hair of the Nandi woman's *piur* grows longer, it is separated into worm-like tufts with fat or red earth: the natural bonnet becomes a shaggy red cap of hide.

Among the Bantu races the beard is usually removed by shaving. The Nandi like to allow the short, sparse beard to remain, especially at the tip of the chin.

The rest of the hair, under the armpits and on the pubic region, which is not at all plentiful, is most carefully removed by both sexes, preferably by plucking out. Among Nandi women this plucking of the hair is done reciprocally.

From what has ben said it can be seen that the black man too has excellently understood how to create new esthetic values for himself by the omission, the shortening or the completing of his growth of hair, which in every way to his mind has an erotic effect. Besides, as in the case of every other ornament, it also serves to differentiate one tribe from another.

29. Women with Skin
Decorations

DECORATION OF THE SKIN

The negro does not seem to be entirely satisfied with
the esthetic feeling which his natural skin affords him. A
fine smooth skin, which we whites wish to keep the same
by the help of all kinds of cosmetics and beauty plasters,
is not exactly the negro's ideal of beauty. He must create
for his skin a new esthetic, *i.c., erogenous* values by painting. oiling or wounding it.

Painting with all kinds of earths, which cannot last
for any length of time, is and can only be applied oc-

casionally. I shall speak of it more in detail when in discussing the ceremonies of circumcision. It can express itself either ornamentally, in that certain extremities of the body are covered with colored decorations, like tatooings (Geluo, Kitosh), or it has purely a coloristic signifi-

30. Girl with Decorative Burns

31. Decorative Burns on Arms and Thigh

cation, in that it gives the dark body a different color, as among the Kikuyu and the Nandi. They rub themselves in, together with their clothing and even their ornamentation, from head to foot, including the genitals, with an earth the color of iron oxide and an animal fat, so that they shine red as copper. This may actually be pleasant,

59

esthetically to us, which does not however mean that the unpainted body is less beautiful. Many are satisfied with simply oiling their bodies with animal fats or vegetable oils; the blending of the different hues of brown of their bodies then appears in full force, like a freshly varnished oil painting.

Since the painting of the body can not be preserved in its immaculate elegance due to the effects of the weather, of bathing and of other rubbing—just look at a black the day after a dance, when pieces of missing clay-like colored earth greatly mar the chromatic unity of yesterday, like sinter in a fresco—it was very natural to make a durable ornamentation to withstand all accidents. Tatooing was resorted to, which, however, has not reached the artistic development as in Oceania. From the point of view of technical execution it is in a very primitive stage; the design is not produced by scratching but by inflaming the skin. This tatooing of the face, especially popular among the Nandi, Lumbwa, Elkoyni, and Kalamega, is purely linear. Usually there are three lines crossing both cheeks meeting in an acute angle pointing towards the nose; but this primitive model may be deviated from when the parallel arms of two angles decorate the cheek at one spot, something like two Roman fives, one shoved inside the other. At times single lines cross the forehead. This simple standard is easily comprehensible when one becomes more closely acquainted with the negro's technique of tatooing. Narrow, delicately smoothed strips of the inner bark of a perennial forest plant, the *jeroryat* of the Nandi, is pasted with spittle on to the skin to be tatooed, and made fast with the thin, inner skin of a hide. This bast has a corrosive effect, and sticks so tightly to the

60

skin, that after a few hours it can be removed only with
the upper layer of the skin, which is what is intended and

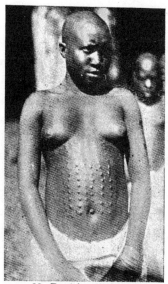

32. Bagisha Girl with
Decorative Scars

33. Baganda with Burns
on Breast

done. But the wound soon heals, leaving behind the scars
wanted. The *black* of this tatooing is not saturated and
almost disappears in the dark brown of Semi-hamitics
face, somewhat like the black spots on the hide of a black
panther, which certainly do evoke an esthetic effect. It
is usually children, between ten and sixteen years of age,
who decorate themselves with such scars. Young people
are often seen with unfinished tatooing, the strips of bast
either pasted on to their cheeks or just torn off; in the

61

last case the line of the wound appears much lighter than the skin, somewhat pale yellow.

Quite peculiar embellishments of the skin are the decorative scars so popular in Africa. Just as the idea of painting the skin may originally derived from accidental soiling of the body with the blood of the slain beast or the conquered enemy, or the intentional smearing of the body against insect bites, so decorative scars may be traced back on the one hand to healed up wounds, caused by men, beasts of prey or hard underbrush, and on the other hand to accidental burns. In both cases the difference in the smoothness and color of the skin was felt to be something beautiful, especially since they must have been tokens of some particular, usually adventurous experience, and so what happened by chance was carefully imitated at home. The accidental now became the intended, the occasional was changed into conscious ornamentation.

Decorative scars fall into two classes: those made by burns and those made by cuts. In these two words is contained the painful technique of the operation to which vain man subjects himself. With pain is beauty bought. This little sacrifice at the altar of the omnipotent god of beauty, however, is suffered without the twitching of an eyelash: rather with pride and forebearance.

I have noticed burns only among the Nandi, less often among the Elkoyni, who abhor scars made by cuts. In boys they are predominantly burned, here and there on the thigh and arm, in girls close together on the upper arm and thigh. They heal over with a gloss; sometimes they are raised, especially on the upper arm, but usually they are on the same level with the skin.

I have watched a Nandi boy during the procedure of burning in a scar (*saryemyet*). He lit with a glowing piece of wood, a piece of dry pith of the plant *tebenguet* (*Emilia integrifolia*) about one-half inch long and gently and quickly fastened it to his thigh. Due to the gentle breeze it began to burn quickly: in an instant only a little ash was left, hot enough to leave a wound behind. The boy was now marked by a burn for the rest of his life, which pleased him far more than the pain he had felt troubled him. On the upper arm of a Nandi girl I counted fifteen such scars set close together.

Scars formed by cutting are very popular and widespread among the tribes of central Africa; perhaps because wounds can be made much more easily, quickly and regularly than burns. Perhaps also because their plastic nature is more in the line with negro taste than the concavity of burns. As was brought out in the discussion of the hip girdle, the sense of touch must also have its erotic finesses. Among women they are much richer than among men. There is hardly a Bagishu, Suk, Kavirondo or Kitosh woman whose body cannot show any number of these ornamental cicatrices. This fashion has a very contagious effect on the women of tribes who are not accustomed to covering their bodies with cuts. It is like that of tatooing from which even an educated traveler in the tropics can hardly keep away, but has his arm or chest pricked by some native, although the style is not exactly the fashion in his own country. I was surprised at the peculiar form of cuts on the face of an old Nyangori woman, which differed from all others known to me: the design consisted of three lines forming an angle, somewhat in the form of the footstep of a crow, and this was repeated several times on both cheeks. I soon discovered that a Nubian woman had cut those scars for her. This standard of design on the face, as well as others observed among the coast population (for example, of Port Sudan) gives one the impression that they are produced by knife cuts.

But I have more exact information on the production of the scars to be found among the Bantu peoples around Mount Elgon. The parts of the skin to be decorated are first raised with thorns from a rosaceous creeping plant. The thorn of this plant which is bent backwards, is anchored in the skin; then it is quickly pulled off, causing a conical protuberance that is immediately cut through with a knife. These wounds always lie in a linear series. I was able to count on the abdomen of a young Bagishu girl, between breasts and navel, eight vertical lines with 94 cuts. All the rows, as well as the whole area that was decorated, were bordered by black lines made with coal and meant to be a protection against the evil eye. I cannot state positively whether all decorative scars are made in this way, especially since the appearance varies considerably. The scars of the kind that I saw among the Kavirondo and Kitosh women were the size of a cherry while those among the Bagishu are about the size of a pea. Differences may also be observed in the plasticity of the cicatrization; while most are more or less raised, some are level with the skin. In the latter case a body thus decorated has a fine esthetic effect; the tips of the scars have a charming sheen in the sun-light, like saturated shadows in purest taffeta (Budama), but the boil-like protuberances running around the forehead of the Kitosh woman to the temples is rather ugly to our eyes. The age of the cicatrization also enters in, since in course of time the unevenness of the scars gradually fade into the smoothness of the body.

The scars are most often produced in the abdomeninal region, but are also to be found on the shoulders, along the ribs (Bagishu), grouped on the back in very pretty lines (Kavirondo) or even around the hips (Suk). But let it not be thought that the scars made by burning and cutting exhaust all the elements of body decoration. First of all there are those tribes among whom inoculation against small-pox is obligatory, which is in all Uganda; and there one finds two or three vaccination scars as large as cherries. Then there are the scars which the black makes on his body for therapeutic purposes, preferably a burn on the temple near the eye (Sebeyi). A Nandi woman even had three somewhat deepened scars, about as large as peas, but very conspicuous, which, she told me, her father had burned in by means of the well known negro tinder, when as a child she lay ill. She had fainted from it. I saw a Nandi with his thigh covered with cut scars as thin as hair. These wounds, hacked in with a sharp knife, had been given him as an aid to convalescence when he was seriously ill. I was struck by the six burns on the breasts of an otherwise unscarred girl given her by a black woman doctor of the village against the *makadja* disease (*elephantiasis?*). The poor child had to be tied down during the operation; medicine was put on the wounds.

Unfortunately the beautiful body of the Nandi woman all too often shows heavy wales on the arms and back—

sometimes as wide as a finger—which attest to the brutality of her husband who beats her with knife and cudgel. Nandi women repeatedly told me this as the cause of such unwanted, tumid ugly scars, and in one case her husband confirmed the truth of her explanation.

If the body of a Nandi woman is examined for its scars, the following cicatrizations may easily be registered: on the temple the burn for therapeutic reasons, on the upper arm and thighs, several oases of ornamental burns, on both arms and calves, the scars resulting from inflammation due to poisoning after the removal of the *segenge,* and finally on the back and upper arm, the thick wales for *pedagogical* reasons. In exceptional cases a little cut scar may be discovered along the edge of the palm of the hand, near the right thumb: this is a sign of blood brotherhood. But more about this later. Among men there is sometimes found a pendant for every decorative swelling obtained through a scuffle, and the possessor may be no less proud of this than the youth of his slashes: I mean the traces of lion or leopard claws, or the large scars received from spears (especially among the Nandi).

The joy in decoration of the body goes so far in many peoples with a marked sense for ornamentation, that they even like to have their cattle covered with designs. For this reason, and probably for magical ones as well, the Nandi occasionally decorate their cattle with burns. The ox shown here is probably the most striking example of this kind of tatooing: one side of it was entirely covered with a decorative design. The present owner, a European, could give me no definite information either on the technique of the tatooing or as to where the animal had come

66

from. But all his men were of the opinion that the "zebra"—that is what they called the tatooed ox on account of the linear cauterizations—had been given those scars by the Nandi. Smaller burns—probably marks of ownership—had been made by markers.

34. Tattooed Ox

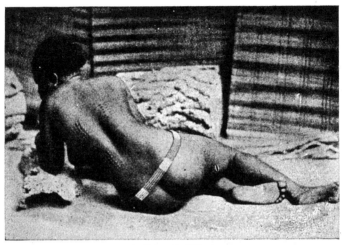

35. Baganda Woman

THE BODY

The body of the blacks appears here in two different types, corresponding to two ideals of beauty. The Semihamitic shepherd and hunting peoples are slender and thin due to their nomadic mode of life and their meager fare; the farmers, however, have a robust body, with a slight tendency towards adipose deposition on account of their rich vegetable food and their heavy work in the field. These two types are not sharply divided; naturally transition forms are found among the massaiized Kikuyu, half shepherd, half agricultural, in whom the tendency towards the robust, the massive, the corpulent is not so marked as in the other Bantu tribes. It is a matter of taste, which of the two receives the palm of esthetic

68

superiority: there Botticelli, here Rubens! There the Semi-hamitic Nandi woman with her tender girl-like form, here the voluptuous Buganda with her Junoesque bosom and soft hips. The thinness of the Nandi woman's calf is partly the result of her *segenge* ornamentation, which cumulatively prevents full formation; on the other

36. Three Virgins—
Center one Bastard

hand, esthetic choice, favored and influenced by the mode of living of these always hunting peoples, has played an important part in producing such tender, often infantile forms. In contrast to the thick and somewhat coarsely formed extremities of the Bantu woman, the arms, hands, feet and legs of the Semi-hamitic mature into such finely

chiselled and beautiful forms, that one is apt to wonder
how the negress attains them, wearing no shoes at all, nor
ever manicuring. The tendency towards flat-footedness,
common among the Kavirondo and Uganda population,
is entirely absent in Nandi women. And such long, slender, neatly profiled, perfectly formed fingers and toes as

37. Elkoyni Girls

the Nandi often has, is not to be easily found even in
cultured Europe. Their husbands also have extremely
slender appendages, showing that they are subject to no
great physical strain.

The negro's stature is of the medium height, not so
gigantic as that of the Nubian and Somali. The woman,

especially the Semi-hamitic, is smaller than her husband.

The breasts of the negress are one of the finest manifestations of the physical beauty of women. In young girls they are hardly noticeable and can be distinguished from those of the coeval boys only by a small elevation around the nipple. At the age of puberty they gradually swell up to a pear-shaped breast, and later into a finely curved, high bosom, which, hemispherical in shape, especially among the Sebeyi and Elkoyni, do not transcend the proportion of Greek canon, in spite of their fresh voluptuousness, exuberant with youthful vigor. The charm of its color is increased by the fact that there is no difference in shade between the breast proper and the region around the nipple, while the breasts of white women often lose too much by the disturbing *negro-brown* of the nipple, no matter how it may be sensuously arousing.

It would be altogether a mistake to imagine that the breast of the negress is always charming and beautiful in its youthfulness. On the contrary, all possible transitions are to be observed, from standing breasts to those limply hanging down, even in girls who have as yet had no children: the breast of the young girl, hardly broken through, is found just as often among adult negresses as are breasts with the nipple almost bent over* (especially among the Bagishu).

Nothing is so transient as the beauty of the feminine breast. And especially in the negress does one often see the rapid passing of the splendid bosom of the girl into

* In Nandis with hard, standing breasts I have sometimes noticed protruding nipples which were bent back like the horns of the chamois.

the formless breasts of the old or middle-aged woman. Women here do not cover their breasts or prop them up in corsets, and hence the drastic effect of nakedness, of the naked truth, which is entirely unknown in Europe. I saw a massaioid Elkoyni woman here who after her fifth child still had passable breasts, and a Mgisho woman, who had already borne six children, with an almost virgin-like,

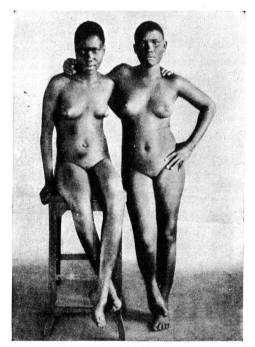

38. Baganda Beauties

well-rounded, hemispherical bosom. Since the child sucks longer at the breast than is customary in Europe, the breasts, thus drawn out, produce more milk than those of the white races, and this is made evident by the volume of the teats, hanging down like oblong gourds. When lactation ceases or draws to its end, these curved, hanging, living milk calabashes assume a somewhat flattened form, which, my black guarantors assured me, were not only not considered to be ugly, but were actually the thing (Kavirondo, Kitosh, Budama). The brass breast plates of the Nandi women, the *taok* described, likewise seem to hasten the desired flattening of the breasts. These flat breasts are fashionable because—as a fair representative of that race excellently explained—a man whose wife has borne him children does not expect or demand of her the appearance of a virgin. The conical milk breasts of the Bantu woman (Kavirondo) are very large; after lactation they are not only flattened, as among the Semi-hamitics, but hang down the upper half of the abdomen. Such hanging breasts of black Catholics have a peculiar charm when a heavy brass crucifix hangs between the breasts on a long chain, and all three, the breasts and the crucifix on the chain of equal length dangle back and forth in walking (Budama).

The breast of the negro, with very little hair, has a tendency among the Bantu tribes to be padded with fat, and together with the plastically protruding nipple, appears bacchical and feminine. The sinewy, athletic form, with its powerful musculature, is rather a rarity here. On the other hand the definitely masculine form of the Semi-hamitic negro approaches that of the semi-hamitic girl, especially in respect to slenderness, symmetry of form and rounding of the arms and legs, although it is naturally much more sinewy and muscular than that of the other sex. In advanced boyhood, however, the chest and abdomen protrudes unesthetically as in the undernourished and becomes ugly if—as among the Budama or Bagishu—the navel projects tumidly from its hollow making the profile of the abdomen irregular and hilly. Such monstrous

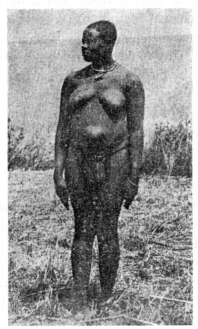

39. Woman with Large
Navel

navels, of which their owners are proud, are also to be found, but less often, among women.

The abdomen of the negress, especially the Semi-hamitic, is very delicately formed, slightly vaulted, and even in women appears maidenly on account of the slender structure of the pelvic girdle. Dependent bellies, disfigured by deep folds, as is only too often seen in corpulent whites in Europe, are entirely unknown here, thanks, in great part, to the hygienic diet of the negress, who eats rather too little than too much. This childlike abdomen passes gently over into the *mons veneris*, which, as a result of but little adipose tissue and a maidenly flatness suggestive of chastity, is not equal to that of the European in tenderness of form. The sparse, sometimes silky hair, which is always either shaved smooth or plucked out, enhances the girlishness of the form.

The *vagina* itself (*kuma* of the Suaheli; *mkolet* of the Nandi), looks somewhat strange on account of its unusual color. Just as the lips of the mouth are not very much differentiated in color from the dark hue of the face, and are lost in a monochrome against the deep brown, and only upon opening of the mouth does the red of the inside of the lips as well as of the gums stand out in full contrast, likewise the vagina and its lips are brown or black externally but rose red within.

And now we have come to the *loca sacre*, as the young Linnaeus once put it. Not only do the genitals of the negress differ externally from those of the European woman by having two marked colors, but there are considerable morphological differences due to artificial manipulation, that may have a corresponding effect on the sensations during the sexual act allowing nuances of pleasure unknown to Europeans.

Two types of vagina are easily distinguished in adult women: that without clitoris (*vagina ankleitoridica*) of the Semi-hamitics and other shepherd peoples, and that with excessively long labia of the Bantu tribes (*vagina hypertelica*). Both forms are produced by artificial treatment: the one by circumcision (Elkoyni, Sebeyi, Massai, Lumbwa, Kitosh, Kikuyu, Kamba) or cauterization (Nandi); the other by direct massaging and partial chemical action on the labia. Characteristic of both types

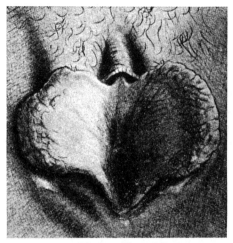

41. Vagina Hypertelica

is a narrowness differing markedly from the European condition, and is not in proportion to the fair size of the masculine organ.

In the chapter on circumcision we shall describe in detail the formation of the *ankleitoridica*—open like a book, "like a door," thus scornfully did a *hypertelic* Uganda woman describe it to me—without any richness of folds, sometimes without a trace of clitoris, and sometimes with a small, hardened, scar-like protuberance after it has been burned out (Nandi). This artificial form presents a clear appearance in the fleshless profile of the labia majora, which from the point of view of fitness must be considered well nigh perfect. Structure here corresponds entirely to function.

In contrast to this ascetic form—if I may term it so—the *hypertelica*, better known by the name of *Hottentot apron*, seems grotesque. Many authors even call it hideous and ugly on account of its color, which ranges from brown to violet. There is no room here for esthetic hyper-sensitiveness: Eros comes before Apollo! In order to intensify sexual pleasure he has come upon the strange idea of forming a vestibule by lengthening the labia and clitoris, to act like a sheath for the entering organ. In profile the labia hang down limply like brown, wrinkled india-rubber bands, when opened they resemble a labiate in form. The negress can stretch this *mfuli*, as it is called in Uganda, to some length, like a rubber band. The length of the *mfuli* is variable, but its minimum is the length of the little finger.

Let it not be thought that the *mfuli* (*bienembe* of the Suaheli) is the exception, produced only by women erotically free and loose. Just as the *ankleitoridica* is a mark of every married woman in the shepherd tribes where it was introduced hundreds of years ago, there is hardly a woman to be found among the Baganda, Bagishu and Suaheli without a *hypertelica* since her youth. Men and women of those three tribes assured me; women without *mfuli* are simply boycotted by men; marriage itself would be annulled if the woman decided to retain her natural clitoris and refused to elongate her labia.

Even before the girl reaches the age of puberty, her mother says to her, "Go, make yourself a *mfuli*." Instructed by older friends, the child now goes into the forest, usually incidentally to gathering wood, takes a weed and rolls it gently with her finger tips in the palm of her hand into a ball, then divides the now yielding material into both hands and busily plucks around both labia with it. With such regular treatment the *mfuli* is ready inside of a week. It is considered ready when it has reached the length prescribed as standard. For this the girl takes a lanceolate leaf of a mintaceous plant, places it on the outside of her little finger and tears off the part reaching above it: the measure is now ready. She then places the leaf against the lengthened labium to see whether the required length has been attained. If not, the plucking is continued (Baganda). If a girl is interrupted during this sexual operation by an impertinent boy and he attempts to crush the "*dava ya mfuli*" (*mfuli* medicine), she implores him to let her alone. "Stop," she says, "if you crush the weed you spoil my *mfuli*."

The Bagishu girls know another method for producing the *hypertelica*. They bind together the plucked labia with a string and have a small stone hang down as a sinker to stretch it properly. "Then the *mfuli* becomes like the crop of a turkey," added a Bagishu woman who was unaffectedly telling me about the operation in the presence of other women.

The origin of the *mfuli* is to be found in masturbation. It was noticed that the labia became elongated: what had been a necessity became a virtue. A man was pleased with such women, especially since continual masturbation had intensified her sex instinct and her sensuousness. As a matter of fact, masturbation is very wide-spread among the Baganda women while it does not exist at all among the adult *ankleitoridic* Semi-hamites. Since in the masturbative lengthening of the labia, an organ was formed that made coitus pleasant and easy, it was but a small step to retain this innovation for ordinary erotic practices. No wonder, then, that the men also seek to keep this practical innovation and refuse to marry women who are recalcitrant and resist this erotic custom.

I do not venture to speak on the morphological structure of the interior of the vagina; it is for a specialist to investigate whether or not it differs from that of the European woman. Its narrowness certainly does speak for a topical difference.*

The *membrum virile* (*mboro*, Suaheli; *pirtit*, Nandi) of the negro is quite large. One sees it all too often, as a result of the inadequacy of his clothing, which hardly covers it (Nandi, Suk, Elkoyni, Tiriki, Bagishu). Every adult without exception is circumcised—only the Uganda boy who has been converted to Christianity in early youth is not. The glans of the circumcised does not differ at all in color from the distal part of the organ; in the uncircumcised it is lighter, somewhat rose-violet. Morphologically it is characterized in being much smaller in proportion to the rest of the cylindriform penis than it is among Europeans. In adults the opening in the glans is open, while in the European it is closed, and it is not bounded off by circumcallation. I could not definitely determine a condition of semi-erection observed by other investigators and described as normal in certain negro tribes.

---

* At any rate the statement of certain authors that the negress is characterized by a roughness of the surface of the mucous membrane which greatly intensifies sexual pleasure, is entirely false. (Vide Remy de Gourmont, The Physics of Love.)

The buttocks of the Semi-hamitic women (Nandi, El-koyni) are very boyish and even in adults finely formed and in no way tending towards steatopyga. Even among Bantu negresses (Kitosh, Baganda, Budama, Kavirondo, Bagishu), who tend more towards retaining fat, with their soft, womanly, Junoesque buttocks, I have never noticed an indication of the hideous steatopyga. Except for her short neck and not especially noble features, the negress is finely proportioned and well formed.

The foot of the Semi-hamite (Nandi) is often very fine, slender and well shaped, the arch especially being accentuated, and unsurpassed by other negresses and hardly even by the European. The robust Bantu are quite a contrast and tend towards flat-footedness as a result of the swampy and loamy country they inhabit. That alone is enough to make the foot clumsy. And since the sand flea is rampant it often happens that one or more toes are missing, giving the foot a hideous appearance. The large visible space between the big toe and the others is probably an indication of its prehistoric mobility in man. Their rhythmical order of the toes is beautiful. The skin of the feet, as well as of the knee, looks like that of an elephant; it is crossed by countless cracks like Japanese crackled earthenware.

As for color, a difference can be distinguished in bathers between those parts exposed to the sun and those covered by clothing. While the torso is chocolate brown (Nandi), the throat and nape, and often the face too, is darker. The armpits are the lightest. Blondes are also to be found occasionally among negroes who are considered very beautiful, and are valued accordingly. They are called *reds*.* They have a much lighter color, brown-yellow, like Creoles. But they are certainly not bastards. Among the Semi-hamitic Nandi, there are two colors: the usual, almost copper-brown, and an almost black skin. Even the Nandi themselves make the distinction and disdainfully call the latter *blacks*.

40. Steatopyga

I asked a copper-red Nandi boy, who was looking at a pretty girl of a darker edition, whether that was his girl,

---

* The negro, as every primitive, has no very copious vocabulary for the designation of colors. Red and yellow, even yellow-brown are the same.

and he answered, "Don't you see that I'm red and she's black? I'll take only a red."

In the preparation of beer the Nandi woman strictly follows this distinction of color. Mixing of spelt and water is done by two women: one mixes, the other pours the water. Both these *bibis* must be of the same color,

42. Kikuyu Boy

43. Massai Man

that is, red and red, black and black. Red ranks higher than black, and the preference of the Nadi for the red paint with which they like to smear their bodies is probably derived, in great part from that esthetic choice of color.

I have also seen albinos; the color of the body was rose-red, somewhat like that of our red heads. The boy in question looked like a European idiot. According to the assurances of my guarantor and companion, the American missionary, Mr. Rees, who had shown me that "wonder of nature," the mental condition of that white negro was not much higher than that of an idiot.

Only the palm of the hand and the sole of the foot differ markedly in color from the rest of the body, being almost as light as that of a European.

The white of the eye is always suffused with a gall-brown color, and so the dark-brown, short-lashed eye of the negress can never shine as beautifully and brightly as that of the European woman.

The typical negro features are the short, stubby, broad nose, pouting, often tumid lips, low forehead, short chin and round face.

The ears are very small, even graceful: perhaps that is the reason why the negro elongates the lobe of the ear so much.

44. Negress

HYGIENE

The negro is in general quite clean. In this respect he
surpasses many a European rural population. No brook,
no lake, no body of water however small is passed without
some negro man or woman bathing, or at least washing.
It is interesting to observe how thoroughly they wash.
Water is scooped up in the hollow of the hand and every
part of the body rubbed well. The soles of the feet are
scratched against stones, the back and shoulder blades,
which are really hard to reach with the hand, are scrubbed

and the stumpy finger nails help in the shampooing of the body. Very often soap is used. Whenever the negro bathes he always washes his cotton garment, and that is why the white negro dress constantly appears clean. Only the shepherd peoples who still retain the leather clothing as described do not wash their clothes, so that the cleanliness of the body is in inverse relationship to that of the clothing. That the negro, be he heathen, Christian or Mohammedan, always washes his hands, which make spoon and fork superfluous, before eating and often after eating, testifies to his cleanliness.

The inhabitants of Uganda wash with a banana sponge (*kigogo*). The pith of the banana blossem is beaten soft and allowed to lie a day covered with banana leaves; the next day the juice of this sponge is used instead of water. The *washing water* of the Nandi women is quite repulsive. It consits of cow and goat urine. Every morning, directly after arising, the hands are rubbed in with urine and then rinsed off with water. If she were to wash her hands with water only, "her husband would die." The men like to have their wives wash their faces with cow urine. "She understands my language," he says to himself when his wife keeps to this primitive cosmetic. There is a bit of superstition in this use of urine as water for washing*. "You get a lot of cattle," a Nandi woman explained to me in full seriousness, when women wash with

---

* Everything from cattle is considered almost sacred. Cow dung is nothing ugly, repulsive, unclean among shepherd peoples. Little children sometimes eat cow dung (Elkoyni); it is used by the negro as cement in preparing mortar, and is also employed as a healing salve in circumcision. After souring milk calabashes are always washed with goat or cow urine and then with clean water. Apparently the saponaceous property of the ammoniac contained in the urine was recognized. Among certain tribes (Kavirondo), cow urine is even added to milk. Thirsty shepherd boys, when lacking water, drink cow urine (Nandi).

goat urine. Usually girls use goat urine and married women cow urine for washing.

Soap is very popular now that it is being imported from Europe in very large quantities or manufactured by Indians and Europeans in Africa itself. The negro even learned how to make soap for himself out of animal fat and the ashes of banana leaves (Baganda), but this era of soap is very recent.

The massaioid Semi-hamites however use only cow dung for certain things instead of soap: with it they polish their metal ornamentation and often rub it into their hands before rinsing them. No wonder, then, that these tribes, who still sleep under one roof with their goats (the majority of the goats, however, sleep with the calves in a separate but neighboring room), smell accordingly. In addition there is the constant exposure of the women to the smoke of the hearth, which likewise leaves behind its peculiar, if not exactly unpleasant odor, so that the smell of a Semi-hamite woman is made up of various components, quite difficult to become accustomed to. But the chord of odors is not yet full-toned: the washed body is anointed with animal fat and the smell of the leather garment polished with fat has its *nota propria*. Boys and girls smear themselves with goat fat, men and women with fat of sheep or oxen (Nandi). However repulsive such a negro woman may smell at first, in time one becomes accustomed to it since the odor is exuded by the leather dress, while the body itself, in contrast to the Bantu tribes, has a not unpleasant odor. The negress of the Bantu races, and the men of those tribes, often exude a nasty, penetrating, undefinable smell which can not be entirely got rid of even after proper soaping of the pores. The

86

introduction of castor-oil, very popular as a salve for the body, probably has something to do with its origin; on the other hand the negro black or brown thereby receives its golden patina. The facts of the odor of the castor-oil are the same as that of the "Nandi-odor" described above: one finally becomes accustomed to it, and in exceptional cases can even call it pleasantly aromatic.

The negro takes exceptionally good care of his teeth. After every meal they are rinsed with water and given a rubbing with the index finger of the right hand. The Nandi employ a toothbrush for this purpose made of an *indigofera* (*mendjeruyet*). The end of a defoliated shrub is chewed until it becomes filaceous and resembles a brush. With this the teeth are rather picked than brushed. Before this procedure the bitter leaves of the same plant are chewed and after a while, when they have ben mixed with saliva, spat out. Other tribes make their toothbrushes from different fibrous stalks (Baganda, Bagishu, Elkoyni, Semeyi). I have seen Massai rub their teeth with wood charcoal and ashes and then rinse them with water. The Baganda use a powder made by crushing pieces of earthenware or kaolin earth. It goes without saying that the teeth consequently look white and healthy. One should think that with this health and beauty of his teeth, man would let it rest at that. But vanity triumphs over healthy common sense: for religious and esthetic (sic!) reasons most tribes break out the two lower incisors with a knife in early youth. The gap thus made, through which the tongue is often seen, looks ugly in even the most beautiful woman.

The teeth of the Semi-hamites are not so well formed as those of the Bantus because they often project quite a bit prognathically and sometimes have interstices between them.

The nails are mostly pared blunt with a knife by men and women and worn quite short (Baganda, Bagishu, Sabeyi). Those of infants are bitten off by their mothers. Both sexes of the Suks wear their nails long and the Nandi men occasionally use theirs to chastise their wives by scratching in addition to their more usual cudgelling.

We have described the body of the black clothed and in all its nakedness; now we will go into the life and desires of the individual: without life, without spirit the most beautiful form is but a husk.

45. Ornaments: a, Kisana;
b, Bracelet; c, Ring

46. King of Elkoyni with
His Wives

SOCIAL DIFFERENTIATION OF THE SEXES

The division of labor between man and woman is much sharper and contrasting among the blacks than with us where a certain obliteration of differences has resulted from the social levelling of both sexes. This very obvious divergence of the positions of the sexes in social life is dictated not so much by the various physiological aptitudes present in both, which, indeed, are fundamentally the same all over—a white woman must nurse her child just as a bush-woman must—and which we shall not treat here, as by the divergent relationship of power under which man and woman live here.

In Africa the man has completely subjected the woman. The working, or rather the slave caste, is recruited entirely from the feminine sex. Consequently the man has rid himself of the heaviest Pariah labor; even that which with us is performed by beasts of burden and trucks, he shoved onto his weaker half, which is just as much his property as any beast of burden.

47. Forest Cleared by Women

But it would be a fundamentally distorted picture if one were to draw the conclusion that it is the woman alone who toils with the sweat of her brow, while the man idly whiles away his life doing nothing. Let one call to mind that all the cultivated ground of the white planter, all the buildings, streets, railroads, bridges, police duty, is the work of living black coal, of the black worker. Without him the interior of Africa would today be still undiscovered in spite of the keen spirit of adventure of its explorers.

Only at home, especially on the reservation, the relationships are shifted. The black worker outside, in his home becomes an employer, a slave-driver, a commander. The woman must chop wood for him, which has to be dragged home from the distant forest or bush. She must fetch water for him—very strenuous work too, when one considers that the settlements are as a rule not situated directly on a stream or spring. The tilling of the soil lies entirely in the robust hands of the woman (Nandi). She is a beast of burden. And how much labor must not be expended in the conversion of the edge of the forest into arable land! It is understood that the woman takes care of all the kitchen work, the washing of the pots and pans and the milk calabashes and keeping the yard clean.

Where the kitchen is a separate hut, as in Uganda, the husband never enters it. The primitive watching of the fire is in close connection with cooking.* Once it has been lit by the husband through friction, it is guarded by the black vestal. While the husband fells wood in the forest for the construction of the hut (it is dragged away by the wife, however), and lays the foundation for his future home by placing posts in the ground next to each

---

* For the relationship between word and concept and the further derivation of a formed expression for the designation of related concepts, it is interesting to bring out that originally "to burn" and "to cook" were one word. In the primitive Bantu language *"gokia'* means to burn, in Suaheli *"koka'* *(oka)* to bake, corresponding to the Indo-European *"quequo"* and the Latin *"coquo"* as an entymological parallel. Similarly, from the primitive Bantu *"kala"* (coal) the verb *"kalinga'* (to roast) is obviously derived. It may be mentioned in this connection that the Finnish has only one verb for "to shine" (of the sun) and "to broil' *"paistaa."*

other either in the form of a circle (Kikuyu, Nandi, all
Bantu tribes) or an ellipsoid (Massai, Elkoyni, Sebeyi),
the wife must see to the rest: the filling out of the walls
with a mortar made of cow-dung and argillaceous earth,
the smoothing out of the floor, the mowing of grass for
thatch and dragging it home. From the preparation of
mortar there arose a new occupation for the woman: that

48. Women as Beasts
of Burden

of pottery, and which in the course of time became the
exclusive* task of the black woman. She noticed that
the crumbling earthen mortar, which was used as a plaster
for the walls, dried out near the hearth into a solid brick-
like material, and during the preparation of food, that
the cracked calabashes that had been mended with clay,

---

* In Africa the art of pottery, from the production of the smallest pipe bowl
to monstrous water receptacles, is in the hands of women. But there are exceptions,
as in Myuma among the Inja, or Msese among the Kampala (Uganda), where men
have become skilfull masters in this feminine branch of industry.

or the baskets smeared with it (like the honey pots even today among the Wandorobbo) received from the fire a hardness that withstood the heat, and it was then made use of in pottery. The potter's wheel is unknown to her. On the other hand, smithery, which among certain peo-

49. Woman Carrying Corn

ples (Nandi, Massai) is actually despised, is exclusively in the hands of the men. The Nandi smith, for example, who is of a tribe other than the Nandi, is said to be allowed to marry only among his own people.

The carving of wood, the laying of traps and hunting, which supplies the family with food, are masculine occupations, as is to be expected. In the care of the cattle there is some division of labor, in that besides the little shepherd, the husband takes over the pasturing of them, the tiresome, daily search for lost members of the herd, and driving them to the salt-lick, as well as inoculating them against cattle-plague; the woman, on the other hand, takes care of the milking and driving the cattle into the stalls and hut over night. The husband does the slaughtering and flaying, while the wife carries home the cut up meat. The stomach belongs to her, the heart belongs to the little shepherd (Nandi).

Beer (*Tembo; Mayek* of the Nandi) is brewed by the women, except for the roasting of the malt (Nandi, Sebeyi). Among the Baganda it is men exclusively who prepare the beloved beverage, never cooking it in the kitchen, but somewheres outside. Beer is an important article of food for the blacks. It is consumed in great quantities. If one considers that all the cultivation of the Eleusine spelt, used principally for this purpose, from the sowing of the seed, the hoeing of the ground (also the only means of ploughing) to the stowing away of the harvest, from the wearisome, laborious stamping of the grains to the malting and brewing of the beer, that all this falls to the busy hands of the woman, one sees what a task she has in preparing beer. According to a legend of the Nandi it was woman who recognized in spelt a plant that could be cultivated. The gist of this story, as the history of most cultivated plants, may be traced back to the discovery of our cereals by woman, a deed not yet fully appreciated.

From the tasks of the woman as described above, we can form a series of pictures showing her at her various daily labors. She is seen in front of the hut stamping spelt in a wooden mortar, or she supports herself with two sticks, like one ice-skating, and for hours, automatically, with her bare feet she stamps grains out of the thick ears (Bagishu). She often makes this task a little more comfortable by sitting down and spreading her extended legs apart which are covered by a skin and crushes the spelt with a stone (Suk). Even more laborious is the conversion of the grains into flour, from which the eternal porridge is cooked (*ugale* of the Suaheli, *kimnyet* of the Nandi). What our windmills and their millstones accomplish, the rubbing stone, day after day, in the indefatiguable hands of countless women must do in Africa. Quite usual is the picture of a woman carrying water on her head in an armless spherical earthenware pot* or in a four-cornered, tin petroleum can, or lugging firewood on her back. Rather reminiscent of Breughel is the woman in her part as mason. The wooden frame-work of the hut is ready. Now the gaping chinks in the walls have to be filled in with a consistent mass of mortar and made into a homogeneous surface, inside and out, by smoothing with the hands. The Nandi woman kneads cow-dung with her hands into a paste for this purpose and carries it into the hut in a receptacle. Inside the half-finished hut the man stands busy weaving a door of switches, as if meaning to symbolize: you work—I watch.

I cannot give any pictures of the man at work, since one can only seldom, if ever, come upon him thus unawares.

It is significant that the baggage-cases of the Nandi, Elkoyni, Sebeyi, woven of switches and bast (*sanandet*), as well as the hampers of the Kikuyu, made of strips of bast and carried with a thong around the forehead represent a typically feminine emblem. No man would carry such a case, not even empty.

---

* The green foliage, which is always to be found inside, is to prevent the possible spilling of the water in carrying.

In the selection of her menu the woman also shows peculiarities, or more correctly, restrictions, unknown to the man, in that she eschews certain foods that are eaten by him. Among men who eat chicken and eggs, grown girls and women will not touch either (Sebeyi, Elkoyni,

50. Woman Stamping Spelt

Baganda). The conjecture of certain ethnologists, that the chicken is holy and rejected for this reason, does not give an adequate explanation why it should be sacrosanct or taboo for the one half and not for the other. The other uncritical explanation, that the man wishes to keep this dainty morsel for himself alone, and keep it from his wife, is not satisfactory either when one considers that among certain peoples (Massai) neither the man nor the woman eats chicken. Perhaps the idea of egg-laying, closely associated with the chicken, is the decisive factor in the aversion of the feminine sex towards chicken flesh, since the woman must be reminded by it of childbirth, which would have the effect of a taboo upon her imagination. Women do not eat the flesh of pregnant goats,

51. Bagusha Stamping
Spelt

sheep and cows, which does not bother the men at all (Nandi, Sebeyi).

The adjuration of lions, as it is practiced here, also gives some suggestion for the understanding of the conception of hetero-sexuality as a taboo for the other sex.

If a Bagishu meets a lion, he approaches it with crossed arms, apparently to manifest his helplessness, and says, "I am a woman and you a man, why do you not leave me in peace? You go your way, I mine." If he were to meet a lioness he would have to present himself as a man, in order that the adjuration does not miss its effect. If he had presented himself to the lion as a man, or to the lioness as a woman, he would have been lost. This course of reasoning indicates clearly that in certain cases, one sex, according to the conception of the Africans, may not or dares not touch the other. For similar reasons, probably, a woman will not drink the blood of a bull or an ox whose blood has been let, while a man, however, will also drink cow blood (Nandi). It is only the male who eats the testicles and the penis of the slaughtered bull, wether, buck or other male animals; it is quite seriously believed that these delicacies increase a man's sexual potency.

The rejection of chicken flesh on the part of the feminine sex, who sees something unclean in the chicken, like the Jew or Islamite in the swine, is to be found throughout Africa. When I had come into a new territory for research, at the Mpolegoma river in Uganda. I once asked the black servant at dinner who was serving roast chicken, whether the woman here ate chicken, and he answered quite vehemently in the presence of all the guests, "Our women do not eat chicken, only whores do!" It is remarkable that prostitutes as a rule eat chicken, while even converted Christian women, of whom the missionary demands, as a sure test of belief, that they eat chicken, break down and soon vomit the morsel which they have only been able to swallow with the greatest repugnance.

Among the Baganda and Bagishu, even among those that are not Islamitic, women never eat pork, which, to be sure, is often rejected by men also. I was also told that in Uganda mutton was eaten exclusively by men. In contrast to this, among the Bagishu, the women eat ape

98

meat. However, only men are said to eat human flesh (Bagishu). The only *food* known to me eaten only by old women, but scorned by the men, are the fat caterpillars of one of the *saturnidae* (probably of a *Bunea* spider) (Bagishu).

Pipe smoking, strangely enough, is much more widespread among women than among men; the men have their snuff and chewing tobacco. In Uganda old women smoke in mourning for their dead children, "in order that they do not worry."

In daily intercourse a certain more or less sharp accentuation of the sex is perceptible: in this respect negro society resembles a synagogue, where men and women are separated as if in two different worlds. Wherever one looks he is met with this social delimitation. Even in going out men and women form two separate groups: girls and women have their circle, men and boys another. If a man goes out with his wife, they do not go out next to each other, but his wife follows behind. Only late in the evening is there a difference: then the woman goes first and her husband behind her (Uganda). Among the Nandi the demarcation between man and women has assumed even sharper lines. The men eat by themselves—usually in the open under a tree—and the women separately by themselves. If they are together the men eat first and then the women take what is left. The men have their own vessels, from which women may never eat (Sebeyi, Nandi, Elkoyni); and the milk calabashes of the men are always much prettier, often beautifully set with beads, sometimes ornamented even with cowrie-shells, than those of their unassuming wives, who skilfully made their husbands' drinking cups. When beer is being drunk, which happens *in gremio,* in a hut, only privileged old women may sit with the men drinkers, while the house-wife must be content with serving the beer she has prepared by pouring warm water at certain intervals into a beer-pot half buried in the floor in the middle of the hut. That occurs so often, that finally the beer is quite weak. Some good natured man, however, when the hour is late, and Gambrinus has begun to have his effect upon the rocking, singing beer bibbers, shuts one eye if an old woman furtively hands the sucking tube to a young one crouching behind her. I have once myself rehabilitated the neglected women in this way. Only the young woman of the house refused to sip beer secretly on the ground that her husband would beat her to death. In answer to the question why his own wife might not drink beer, while the fine beverage was not denied to utter strangers, a man said to me: if his wife got drunk, who would then fetch wood all night, heat water all the time and keep pouring it into the beer?—arguments, which from the point of view of his other acts of subjugation towards his wife, sound quite plausible. If a senescent woman who has no fullgrown children can not very well by herself do all the work of clearing, sowing and cultivation, her husband is consulted as to whether some of the neighboring women should not be called in to help. He has no objection, especially since beer drinking is then indispensible. So all the men of the neighborhood who are ready to have their wives help, are invited, but their wives stay right at home and work (Nandi). The women brew for themselves a kind of small beer, which ferments in six days instead of eight, contains no alcohol, and is drunk only by women and

100

children. It is called *mosarek* and made of Eleusine grain (Nandi).

Among the Nandi only the husband or his high guest may sit on the low round chair, of which there is only one in the hut, never his wife.

52. Girl at Work

Even in everyday expressions there prevails among the Semi-hamitic shepherd peoples a certain differentiation between men and women: the women are greeted differently from the way the men are, and also answer the greeting differently. *"Takwenya"* is said to the woman of the Nandi, Elkoyni, Sebeyi or Massai, who answers *"Igo"* with strong accentuation. But the circumcised man or old man is greeted with *"Subai!"*, to which the answer *"Ebo!"* is received. But it is more remarkable that the women of a tribe will answer every call with a word that is different from what the men will use. A falsetto-like, fine sounding, long drawn out *"E-e-e!"* is the usual

answer to a call. Girls, even little boys, likewise answer
in this manner. In a similar case the man grumbles his
"Uy!" to himself.

Boys, youths and unmarried men have their own huts
(*sygraynet*) constructed differently from the usual ones
for the simple reason that they do not have to be divided

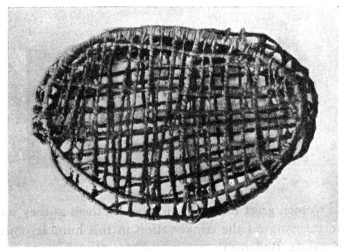

53. Basket

into two rooms, one for the accommodation of cattle,
which never pass the night there. They build the huts
themselves; girls do the masonry work and women fetch
the necessary hay for thatch (Nandi).

Most conspicuous are the different ways in which men
and women sit, a differentiation found already in early
youth. The man crouches (his feet are not crossed, as is
the oriental fashion, nor are they stretched out); usually
his buttocks do not touch the ground. The ancient Egyp-

102

tians have masterfully preserved in their stone statues this crouching position, which was general then. The woman, on the other hand, never sits in this position*, but actually touches the ground with her buttocks and stretches her legs out straight in front of her, or kneels on both knees. In Uganda this is even the manner in which girls

54. Bachelor's House

and women greet men, kneeling before them as they stand and carrying on the conversation in this humble posture (Baganda, Budama).

On the other hand it is quite remarkable that the posture of men and women when urinating is the same. Both discharge this function in a crouching position. The reason will be discussed in another place (Nandi). The men are not at all ashamed of doing it in front of their huts in the presence of the women, while a woman would not do it in public.

There is a differentiation in the gait of both sexes also,

---

* Nandi women have explained the reason to me. Their sexual parts would be seen if they crouched in that position. A man does not care if a woman sees his penis, but a woman hides her genitals; probably for magical reasons.

103

especially among the shepherd and hunting peoples: the men walk somewhat bent forward, throwing their body forward like a wading bird; the women tend toward a bow-legged posture in walking and standing, so that the feet are often thrown outward in the first case, and directed inward in the second. Among the Bantu the gait of the women seems rocking and dragging.

As is to be expected from her occupation with bead-embroidery, the sense of color is much more marked in women than in men.

In respect to the practice of music the relationship is reversed. The man appears to be the musician in song and dance. The woman, on the other hand, really plays no instrument. But there are two exceptions. Like the lute, the primitive, five-stringed harp, without a sounding-board (*ubungadet* or *kipokandet* of the Nandi), played on a cow-hide or some other substitute for a sounding-board, is also played by women, especially by prostitutes. The only instrument known to me that is exclusive property of the women is the elegant zither made of reeds (*ditungu*), which looks like a pipe of Pan. Its tone, brought forth by a plucking of the reed strings with the finger-nails, is weak, somewhat like that of a musical box. As with the Nandi-harp, Bagishu girls amuse themselves with it for hours, strumming a melody that is not very rich, or rather, simply a few notes. Sometimes girls also beat the drum, but more through arrogance than the desire for rhythmical expression. However, they never do it at the dance. Among the Baganda an old woman beats the drum in mourning, especially if there are no men present to do it.

Otherwise it is the man who beats or plays the drum, the guitar (*kinanda*), the *katingeti* (one-stringed fiddle of the Baganda), the shepherd's flute (*ndenge*), the large horn. It is he who sets the time, rhythm and melody at

55. Kneeling Girls

the beer carousels, while only in exceptional cases an old woman makes herself noticeable at intervals by interrupting in a shrill, falsetto-like voice.

At the dance the man makes the music. Here the two, otherwise separated sexes meet, old and young. Here is the place where the women can show her physical beauty to all. Even among the Christianized Baganda, where it is usually considered repulsive to bare the breasts, the full bosom is now shown. Men and women do not dance together, as with us. Near each other, they go through their rhythmical motions, staying in one spot all the time. Here they hop, stamp and jump. The hips, abdomen and

105

bosom describe a rocking, shaking, reeling movement, the outstretched arms and hands help along, at times strongly resembling the sexual act. Among the Nandi, where men and women do not dance together, but only in close proximity, the dance-forms of the feminine sex are quite different from those of the men. While girls and women stand in a row or in a circle, singing gaily, gently swaying their legs to and fro, and beating with their swinging hands on their leather clothing, the men do actual high-jumping so that one is reminded rather of gymnastic exercises than of dancing.

And as in every dance, everything is in the service of Eros.

56. Family Idyll

THE RELATIONS OF THE SEXES TO EACH OTHER

Forced by social conditions and driven by inborn desire to travel, the masculine youth leave their reservations, situated at some distance from the European plantations, at the early age of about twelve years. The pasturing of the cows and goats since the age of five, helping their mother with cultivation, all non-remunerative labor, arouses in them the longing for change, for other conditions, and especially for money. They wander to the white man to earn bread from him, or more correctly, the eternal, pasty, *ugale* (porridge) cooked from corn meal (*posho*). He now puts on the straight-jacket of service, which never fits exactly, as errand-boy, carrier, ox-driver, factory worker, cook, farm hand, in short, as a *boy*. If he has not felt the influence of the missions before, he now gradually becomes externally Europeanized, and this shows itself at first in his scorn of his former clothing, often lack of clothing, and his procuring little

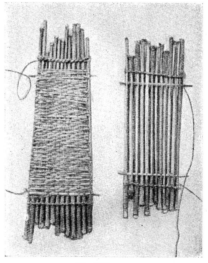

57. Ditunga

by little, single articles of European clothing. He begins with the short linen or khaki trousers.

From time to time he is visited. His feminine relatives come also, with whom occasionally one of his comrades forms an intimate acquaintance. Many of them are of a passing nature, many lead to marriage. Now he must save, to defray the dowry, which is given in the form of cows, goats and similar primitive methods of payment. When he has saved some money, he sends it through one of his

108

brothers, as he calls even his most distant relative, to his father, who, by purchasing cattle, starts his future capital. If he thinks he has now served enough, he hurries back to his village, free and spurred by home-sickness, where in the course of time he arranges about the pur-

58. Nandi Dancing

chase price of his future wife. It may then happen that a *boy* has not collected the whole sum. If his father does not wish to, or cannot lend it to him, his father-in-law gives him credit, which is always paid off to the last penny. If a son-in-law were not to pay back this debt of honor, his children would "die one after the other" until he had paid it all back. Among certain tribes the son-in-law must replace the stipulated cattle for his father-in-law in case they perish, even many years after the wedding.

Only a small percentage of the masculine negro youth

109

spend their storm and stress period, the time between boyhood and manhood with the white man, far from their
parental home. Most of them remain close at home,
where they have farming and shepherd work to perform,
but which they gladly devolve upon their younger brothers
and sisters, who are to be found in every kraal, so that

59. Bowman

they may revel in *dolce far niente*. They play, shoot with
bow and arrow, hunt, and of course dance in the evening.
Everyone has a little affair from his tenth year (Nandi).
It is favored and furthered by the institution of the war-

riors' or men's house (*sygraynet*), according to which, from childhood on, no unmarried male person may sleep in the parental house. No father will tolerate an older child in his hut. The girls also must sleep somewheres else, usually in the house of their *other mother*, unless papa himself happens to be staying there, or, in case their father has only one wife, with some near-by aunt. Now the girls sing, dance and are happy because they are rid of the difficult work of keeping the house in order and seeing to the cow stalls. Boys visit them, entice them out, arrange a rendezvous, and in the men's house the young negro's flirtation finds its natural conclusion; if it has not already been finished out in the open.

Public opinion, if there is such a thing, does not really bother so much about this loose, lascivious, unbridled life as the unmarried men themselves, who feel themselves justified in exercising a certain moral jurisdiction. Jealousy is also a factor in many cases, since the girl with whom the young uncircumcised boy (*layoni*) is flirting is often the sweetheart of a man (*moran*). The honor of the warrior (*moran*) cannot bear or tolerate it; that anything so inferior as one uncircumcised, a boy, should decorate himself with rich ornamentation, and even make advances to girls. When they meet such boys, they give them a good beating and take away their ornament, money, arms and cap.

Close by my quarters there took place one night a gruesome scuffle which clearly shows the procedure of this *moral police*. A great number of *layoni* had met in a hut for a dance. A band of warriors appeared, locked the boys in the hut, and at first wanted to smoke them out. It was not until the mother of one of the *layoni* came

111

hurrying by and spilled milk out of a calabash onto the ground as a sign of an intense plea for mercy and forgiveness that the *morans* were finally pacified. Some of the *layoni* had previously been given a good beating. All this was a punitory expedition against certain boys who had too often seduced the girls of the neighborhood (Nandi).

60. Kyepta with Osyek

61. Boys Before
Circumcision

CIRCUMCISION

It is not until one is circumcised, becomes a warrior
(*moran*), as he is called among the shepherd peoples, does
he enjoy full freedom of deed and action, a freedom
which he uses especially for erotic purposes. Uncircumcised he cannot and may not marry; the same is true for
the bride among the shepherd and hunting peoples. It
is only through circumcision that society declares them
adults, sexually mature. Therefore nothing is more desired by the negro boys and girls than to have gone
through circumcision, which for them is a milestone in
social position between two stages of life: the boy (*layoni*)
becomes a man (*murenin*), the girl (*kyepta*) becomes a

113

woman (*osotya*). Thus they become new people. Affectionate, infantile names become invalid from now on; the new name which they receive remains with them to the end of their lives (Nandi).

In spite of the wide diffusion of circumcision among most peoples, nothing definite is known about the reason for it. If one asks a native about it, he says either, "*zamani!*" (with a long drawn out emphasis of the "*ma*), which means "since ancient times," or he answers that it is just a custom: neither one of them an explanation.

The reason given me repeatedly, for the circumcision of girls among the Nandi, was that the children of the uncircumcised would die. But that is an inference drawn from the existing inhuman custom of strangling the children of uncircumcised girls. So this is no explanation either.

In answer to my question on the circumcision of girls a village chieftian said to me, "We are Nandi, we don't want anything hanging like that in the front of our women!" And he made a disdainful gesture with his little finger, as if he meant to signify the clitoris. Without doubt the circumcised genitals of men and women are considered beautiful. Circumcised as well as uncircumcised have constantly assured me of that. However high one wishes to put the negroe's marked desire for beauty, still it does not seem to me to be enough for one to postulate that the origin of circumcision is purely esthetic. Nor is it due to magical-religious reasons. Hygienic motives cannot have been decisive, since circumcision in many races occurs many years after repeated practice of sexual intercourse. It seems to me that the fundamental reason for circumcision can easily be inferred from the nature of sexuality.

Man strives to make the often troublesome act of intercourse as comfortable as possible; and it cannot be denied that the foreskin is often a painful hindrance, becoming strangulated after the entrance of the glans and

62. Layoni

making the act difficult, or in case the prepuce does not leave the glans free, hastening the *ejaculatio seminis*. What could be simpler than to do away with this hindrance, especially since an additional mark of beauty is thus attained for life.

And of secondary significance are the months of convalescence following the operation, when the youth, now a man, can find opportunity, lacking schools, to be initiated by his master into all the mysteries of life.

For the circumcision of girls there are other reasons. From her eighth year onward a girl is common property. Anyone who has any command of masculine eloquence can have her. Very small girls sleep with boys of their own age, the older ones, about twelve years and above, are never scorned by unmarried warriors. The parents do not interfere in these little love affairs; they have no opportunity to learn anything about them, since the girls as well as the boys do not sleep at home, and what with the prevalent prudery, which forbids even the hinting of anything repulsive or indecent in the presence of the parents, no one tells them anything about it. If the young lovers are caught by their parents *in flagranti,* there's a licking received, to be sure: the boy runs away, the girl gets the blows. And that's the end of the matter. Through marriage the girl becomes the property of her husband. Now she cannot give herself to everyone openly, and every *layoni* especially bewares of seducing the young wife or any other *osotya.* Circumcision, which, as has already been mentioned, confined to the clitoris, sets a barrier to the mad life of the girls. Whereas formerly common property, she is now a private possession. Circumcision is the symbol of the change of possession. The practical significance is primarily that of withdrawing the convalescent girl for some time from the obtrusiveness of the young people. But the real reason above all is that of removing the erogenetic zone from the front into the vagina by the extirpation of the organ most sensitive for the *libido sexualis,* and of bridling her lasciviousness in order to force upon her in this manner a monagamy that is repugnant to her nature. And there is good reason for the

116

fact that she does not have to work during her period of convalescence, but simply battens: she is to be made as strong as possible for the physiological function of bearing a child, which is soon to occur.

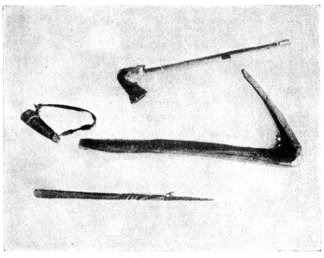

63. Circumcision
Instruments

Society pronounces the death sentence upon illegitimate children, as those of the uncircumcised are considered. They are choked to death by their mothers (Nandi).* In small market towns, or in cities where the police know everything, such deeds are not dared to be done. There the mother lays the new-born child in front of the door of her hut. An acquaintance, usually a childless prostitute, takes pity on it and brings it up.

---

* Usually the throat of the new-born babe is stopped with cow-dung.

Illegitimate children are not tolerated at all among the Nandi and other shepherd peoples; they are got rid of (for a motive similar to that of the infanticide among us) in order not to offend the morality dictated by the community.

64. Pantomine of the Sebeyi

Those being circumcised are nearly of adult age: it is therefore painful. What must not a boy or girl go through before undertaking this extreme mutilation? First the upper margin of the ears were pierced, then the lower incisors were broken out. Then it was the turn of the ear lobes, when the pains of the enlarging of the aperture certainly were worse than that of perforation. The abdomen, back, thighs and arms were tortured by cicatriza-

118

tion with fire or knife. For the last pain—that of circumcision—the body has been adequately hardened.

Circumcision of the youth takes place about the fourteenth year; of the girls somewhat earlier. Any day of the year is suitable for the circumcision of girls—they

65. Candidates for
Circumcision

are circumcised any time their parents or future husbands care to—but the time for the circumcision of the boys has been set decades in advance. Among the Nandi it takes place every four and a half years. The next time will be in the spring of 1934. The recruits of various years convene for that solemn act of life: it is undertaken in common. The circumcised class has its name which

119

binds the members together for ever, like those of a col-
lege class, indeed, even in a sort of blood relationship.*

There is much dancing the evening before. *Layoni* and
morani appear in their copper-red paint. They enliven

66. After Circumcision

the monotonous red of their bodies by parallel or wave-
like streaks on their legs and arms, formed by skillful

* A woman may not cohabit with the circumcision colleagues of her father;
i. e., those of the same class (Nandi).

120

scratching away of the paint so that their black skin background appears. Ornamentation and headdress is in keeping with this prelude to the operation. They dance, leap and hop until they are exhausted.

Very early the next morning the candidates for circumcision appear in pompous dress. They have borrowed brass plates, a string of beads for the ear (*muita*) and a ring for the neck (*merenget*) from the women; around their necks and in their ears they wind garlands of a *ficus* variety. They have just returned from the river whither the master, their circumcisor (*Materyot*) had sent them before sunrise to bathe. *"Lapat iun,"* "Go wash it," he has said to them. They had gone there, drawn the fore-skin back, and washed the member. The master looked on. Now they return to the forest, where circumcision always takes place. No one who is uncircumcised, no feminine person or animal may be present. *Morani, boyot* (the old men), and those to be circumcised gather around the burning pyre. Now an old man comes. He questions the boys as to whether they have ever had sexual intercourse with a circumcised woman,—the uncircumcised do not count. Then the poor fellow must confess. He must look into the face of *Asista,* the sun, his god: this is as binding as the swearing of an oath. Great suspense predominates. The excited *morans* listens to this confession with anxiety because there is always the possibility that one of them will publicly learn that he has been horned. The latter goes home afterwards and beats his wife dead. The candidate for circumcision behaves quite ungallantly: without pangs of conscience he sacrifices in front of all, the woman he seduced, to shame and beatings. If he likes her he says something like, "I loved with her and slept with her in the open."* He is not bothered now by the fact that he has promised her never, under any circumstances, to betray her name. But if he is indifferent to the woman, he says something like, "I went into the forest and she called me to her, although I did not want to at all." It is under-

67. Kitosh Boys Just
After Circumcision

standable why married women, even those that prostitute themselves, have nothing to do with *layoni* in the face of such a scandal.

Now the fire in the pyre crackles. An iron staff is glowing in it, the *medyeuta* resembling a chisel, with which tatooing or the sign of ownership is usually branded on cattle. On a bench a brother or an old man mixes crushed, white clay with milk, which is then rubbed into

* To sleep with a woman in the open is not so bad as in a hut.

the head of the candidate who crouches on the ground. Now comes the *materyot* with his assistant. They sieze the drawn out foreskin, the one holds it fast, the other

68. Arbor of the
Circumcised

takes the glowing iron and passes it around the fore-skin till it falls off charred. The assistant throws it away while the master, with a little stick, applies fat from the udder of a cow to the wound. During the whole operation the candidate must not cry out, or it would cost him his life. He would be mercilessly pierced through with a spear if he cried out.

Now the newly-circumcised (*tarusyot*) withdraw into the boys' hut (*mendjet*) especially built for them. This

69. Circumcision Song

hut is quite crude, without any kind of plastering, and becomes the abode of the circumcised for several months. A little child brings them their food: milk, porridge and sometimes meat. Their fathers, the old men, morans and boys come to greet them. Their clothing consists of a tightly fitting cow-hide (*goryet*). If by chance they should meet a woman in the forest, they must quickly cover their faces with foliated twigs.

The *materyot* remains with them. He initiates them into all the mysteries of life. They must make themselves an immense head-dress of palm leaves and a mask, the *kimarangochet*, with which the master helps them. Birds are shot with the bow and arrow; the master receives the flesh, the skin is smoked and drawn around the mask. Thus they go about during the last part of their conclave.

. . . in the meantime the wound heals.

If it has not yet healed completely, the *tarusyot* is told

something like the following by his mentor, "If you are not yet whole, do not go into the forest; you will meet a woman there and your organ will be ruined. I shall not make it good for you. It is good that you go to your parents, that they may make it whole for you."

After about three to six months of this luxurious life, when he has fully recovered, the *tarusyot* finally leaves the boys' hut. The *materyot*, as before mentioned, has given him all kinds of rules of life, how he is to conduct himself towards women, what he must do in case a cow is about to calve on the way to the salt-lick, or he has given him lectures on the healing power of certain plants. Many questions are now put to him. For example: the *tarusyot* goes on the day of the examination to bathe in the river. A spear is stuck in the bank. The bather sees only the reflection of the spear in the water. "What is that?" asks one of the *morans*. "A spear," is the answer. "Indeed, how he knows," says his rejoicing friends.* Now he goes into the water again, all besprinkled him with cow urine that they have brought along in calabashes, examine his healed organ, and then go. He follows them clothed in a mantle of black ox-hide. There is dancing. Women and children come to stare at him. "Where is the child of Ar-ap so and so?" they ask joyously. He is pointed out; he extends his hand in which he is holding an especially fine bow and arrow and belt to a girl.

In the meantime the beer at the *materyot's* is ready. It is dark. Then the people show him more things. A lion comes and roars, "guh, guh." He trembles with fright.

---

* Hollis gives another question, ("What resembles the sound of the vagina during coitus?" Answer: "The gentle rustling that hisses over the fire.") but which was not given to my candidate.

But soon he becomes angry, because he sees that the people have been fooling him. They come and show him an earthenware vessel. "What is this? they ask. "A pot," he answers. "That is the lion," is what he now hears. All drink beer. He does not because it is the beer that his mother has prepared for him; it now belongs to the guests. The next morning he is a free man. The master takes him into the forest and cuts his hair close about his temples. He adorns his forehead with glass beads, and the rest of his body with breast-plates (*taok*) and many kinds of ear pendants, puts on an ape skin, takes a bow and sets out. If he passes huts in which there are women he calls loudly, "Ch!"; then the girls and women come to him, give him their hands and offer him milk and other food outside. Then he goes into the *old men's house*. His girl comes. At first he pretends to sleep. She stays with him all night. Early the next morning she gives him her hand in parting and says, "I shall come again in the evening and will then give you my vagina. My dear sir! It is now that I really love you; I will now have myself circumcised too, then you will buy (marry) me, to take me away." Then he goes to his mother; not through the main door but through the back entrance of the half of the house that is set aside for the goats and calves. His mother at first gives him milk mixed with blood to drink, later she offers him porridge and milk. Now he looks at his goats. Not until the evening does he go out through the main door. The next day his friend visits him and he slaughters a goat for him. The day after his friend slaughters one for him. They eat—the goat's stomach is given to his mother.

The loafer now has his day all to himself. He is free (Nandi).

The Nandi are the only people known to me who circumcise boys and girls by burning (circumbustio); everywhere else the knife is used for this purpose.

Among the Elkoyni circumcision is performed in the presence of all, even of women. The operation is introduced by dancing. The boys dance, the old men drink beer. Before sun rise the youth takes his bath in the river, returns to the hut and besmears himself with white clay if he has no red. His head is smeared with loam. The *old man*, who performs the circumcision for a fee of a goat and one or two shillings, spreads out the cow-hide outside of the hut. He takes hold of the fore-skin of the standing youth, draws it back, and smears loam between it and the glans; then his assistant draws it far down again, presses his nail around into the protuberant skin and holds it tight while the old man cuts it off with a knife. The assistant then improves the cut somewhat with the knife. The circumcised does not blink an eye-lash. The men help him sit down while the old man carries the fore-skin and the blood caught in the cow-hide into the forest; the cow-hide is later brought back and washed clean of blood with ox fat. The boy's mother comes, brings her son milk and anoints him with ox fat. A *moran* attempts to smooth the wound in the foreskin by removing excrescences with a long thorn. Now the *old men* drink beer till late at night while the young men outside perform their jumping dances.

If the boy has cohabited just before circumcision and bleeds too profusely, then the woman he possessed, and whose name he makes known, must give him a piece of her clothing to wear as an amulet. "Otherwise the bleeding would never stop!"

The circumcised then retire for several months, like the Nandi, in their boys' hut.

One of my boys, who was about thirteen years old and had already been circumcised, told me the following about the circumcision of the Sebeyi: Every boy longs to be circumcised. Why? Because it looks fine and the women will have sexual intercourse only with those that are circumcised; the uncircumcised *uerit* are simply boycotted by the women. The one to be circumcised, whose head and chest are smeared with the contents of a bull's stomach, stretches out his arms towards the sky in a standing posture, in his hands he holds a staff parallel with the ground, while two men (in the manner of the *elkoy- ni*) circumcise him. The fore-skin (*sumsumyet*) and the bloody earth is kept together with the grass. The youth must now sleep near it for three days. Only then may he throw everything away in the forest. The circumcised may not sleep in his parental house but in a hut especially constructed for the purpose. Everything that the convalescent touches he must first spit on three times and then touch it lightly as if only feeling it. His mother may not visit him during this time, nor may they look at each other. If she happens to pass by she covers herself entirely with her dress and hastens away into the bush. The boys and girls visit him and inquire about his health. After three months, when the hair that has been cut short before circumcision has grown again, he may leave the hut. Before doing this his mother rubs his head in with ox fat. All *morans* now greet him with "*Subay*," whereupon he self-consciously answers "*Ebo*." Now he may sleep with every woman that offers herself to him, although he is so young that he has no ejaculation. He is the darling of the women!

Another circumcised Sebeyi boy supplemented this description: Right after circumcision he jumps into the air with outstretched arms, the staff in his hands, moves his hands up and back, until the old man slowly helps him to the ground. Everyone dances around him while he shakes his head from side to side in satisfaction. Now his mother gives him milk, bringing the calabash to his mouth in zig-zag motions and every now and then spitting gently. He drinks, presses his knees together, and takes care that no drop of milk fall upon his penis or "the glans would fall off." His friends give him presents, he strings his money on the women's neck rings that he has on, like the diadem described before. After three days a *moran* brings him warm water for bathing. At most in four months he is recovered. He then leaves his hut on all fours. He discards his leather frock, with the typically feminine girdle of cowrie-shells, for the men's dress, in his hands he holds a staff and a cudgel. He beats with it while the youth dance. They dance in this way for four days from one hut to another. Everywhere he is offered milk, everywhere he receives fat for anointment. When he has his hair cut and goes far away with his comrades to hunt the she-antelope. *"Akore moran!"* "I am a *moran!"* he cries beaming with joy and pride when he has dispatched a she-antilope with his cudgel. He is ridiculed if he returns without game. When he returns to the house of his parents, his mother embraces him with the words, "My child, now he has got game!"

At the end of their life of seclusion, the circumcised execute a very remarkable dance, which looks rather like a pantomine, and which was never before recorded. Boys and girls gather together for the dance. One of them carries a crude, oblong shield, woven of switches. He takes a position as if for single combat with another who bears a whip. The latter lets fly at him as he crouches behind the shield. He cannot parry and falls over in fun,

70. Lumbwa Girls Decorated
for Circumcision

whereupon the rest of the youth cries, like an antique chorus *"Kame!"* "He is dead!" Then the one who has been vanquished arises and takes the whip, the victor takes the shield, and they repeat the same play as harmlessly as before (Sebeyi).

Among the Kitosh circumcision is performed in a similar manner. The candidate, who first rings cow-bells, and then goes about bedaubed with flour, the contents of an ox's stomach and mud, and all kinds of meat around his neck, sits down for the operation. It is similar to that of the Elkoyni. During it one of the spectators flings a cock over the roof, whereupon all present call out in jubilation "siririri na-a-ah!" The circumcised disappears into the boys' hut.

It is similar among the Bagishu. The candidates dance, stamping their feet, until they are exhausted, ardently singing their song of circumcision. It is said that even after circumcision the intoxication of dancing comes upon them and they keep stamping their feet. Some brave fellows do not have the fore-skin circumcised all at once, but in two parts: the upper part one day, the lower the next. If one can imagine this courageous deed, one sees why in some tribes, as among the Kikuyu, it may finally come to the point where all the men are only half circumcised, the lower part of the fore-skin not being removed at all but left hanging for the rest of their lives. "The Kikuyu has two organs," says the neighboring tribes. This hanging fore-skin is a hindrance to sexual intercourse. I was told that the Kikuyu, as a result of this loose skin, could not enter at all. Only after his wife had had a child is complete copulation possible. His fore-skin hanging down in front of the *ancleitoridica* is supposed to be capable of being very arousing to the woman during coitus on account of the displacement of the centers of desire by extirpation.

Among the Akamba, who, as Islamites, are circumcised

131

very early, the bleeding is stopped by applying the excrement of the red-headed lizard. The parents, who are not present, prepare beer and food in the meantime.

The Maragoli, during circumcision, hold a staff with both hands tightly pressed against their backs, in order not to move or writhe during the operation.

71. Nandi Thigh-Belt

Circumcision of the boys cannot be suppressed even by the missionaries—perhaps because the Mosaic belief approves of it—but that of the girls is vigorously combatted by the missionaries, in which they are supported by the government. The government cannot prohibit it entirely, the custom is too deeply ingrained among the shepherd peoples. Through education and prosecution, however, it is believed that this brutal custom, which is in no way more barbaric than circumcision of men, can be gradually abolished. For example, in the district northwest of Victoria Nyanza, I have been told by missionary, the captain of the district tried to combat circumcision of girls on his own responsibility by introducing large fines for it. The one who performed the operation had to pay 50 shillings, the one who was circumcised 25. This fine was divided between the chieftian of the village in question and the state. The fact that the sultan of the village received so much money from these fines that he could buy himself an automobile, clearly shows that the negroes will spare no sacrifice to be able to retain their national, erotic peculiarities.

Girls are seldom circumcised before their twelfth year —after the appearance of the pubic hair—but rather later.

I was told of a mother-in-law who found out that her son had married such a "hairless" woman, she became half insane. She went into the bush, sat there four days without food among the rambling hungry hyenas, who kept circling around their prey. In this condition, more dead than alive, she was found by the police chief, Mr. Ruscoe. The grass around her was quite crushed by the beasts of prey. He took her to her hut, had the father-in-law give the son back his dowry, and take back the young woman. The old woman recovered—the young one probably became a prostitute.

The circumcision of the girls (*tundu*) among the Nandi

133

is an operation without equal. Preparations are made for
it several days in advance. Those to be circumcised must
first borrow their ornamentation from their friends. As
the boy for his circumcision shone in feminine ornament,
the girl now on the longed-for day appears in masculine
adornment.

72. Circumcision Costume

73. Materyot

The calf-skin for the buttocks (*goysit*), the snuff-box
(*kivraut*), the fine mantle of the old people, consisting
of square cow-hides sewed together (*kibvet*), the horse-
tail (*gotyat*), the cudgel (*nyarit*), all these are borrowed
from *morans* and old men for a short time. They all part
willingly with them, for they know that the girl, in the
most sacred hour of her life will not cry out, but cour-
ageously bear the pain. If she were to cry out, every one

134

of the men, from whom she had borrowed the ornament, would throw them away in disgust instead of taking them back, her father or brother might even kill her with his spear. The ornamentation is not yet complete, the strange-est, most singular, most original part is missing yet—the thigh-bell. A massive iron bell, 6 inches long, the *kur-*

74. Girls Just After
Circumcision

kuriet, looking like a monstrous, half open pod, from which about five iron peas peep out like teeth, and which hangs down on a strap decorated with beads and set with cowrie-shells, is yet to be got. Preferably six of them: three on each leg; the more bells the louder the noise made by the rhythmic shaking and stamping. This orna-ment, as well as his high baboon-skin cap, is worn only once a year by the *moran.* It was used originally to scare-up beasts of prey (lions and hyenas) when hunting. But now its only purpose is for lending it to girls at the circumcision festivals. Of her own ornamentation the girl wears her fine fringe apron (*osyek*), the fillet (*kilisik*), with or without *songonyet*, and all kinds of neck rings, borrowed from her mother and aunt. The wooden ear-blocks are set on their cut surfaces with a circle of beads.

75. Infibulated Vagina

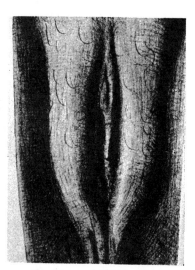
76. Circumcised Vagina

The head is anointed, a cross bar is drawn with coal over the forehead. The men and women who appear at the operation are dressed in their finest ornamentation. They do not want to be surpassed by the bride in magnificence; they are adorned with red earth, neither are the black stripes, mentioned above, loking like stockings with long stripes, lacking; they are anointed with oil and fat, so that the red color runs over their foreheads from the tops of their heads. There is wild dancing all night long. *Stolen water tastes sweet*: it is as if this night had been made for adultery and other love affairs.

The next morning before sunrise a fire is made in front of the hut and next to it is a little tree planted there for this purpose. The ceremony takes place here. Here the parents bless their child. The day before an old woman had already fetched in her leather clothing the fiercely burning stinging nettles (*siwot*) of the *Girardinia condensata*. In the evening the girl sits on the four-legged stool, on which otherwise no feminine creature may sit; she spreads her legs apart and her genitalia are examined —her mother is not present—carefully and searchingly. If it is found that she is a virgin, she is kissed by the women; all are happy: indeed her father even has a cow slaughtered when he hears the good news! The nettles are now applied to the clitoris (the *kabinyet* of the Nandi and Elkoyni). It burns infernally, but the child bears the pain with unbelievable patience. The clitoris swells and becomes large. That night the girl falls asleep with the thought: tomorrow there is an even greater pain, and then I become a woman, a wife, a mother.

It is to take place early in the morning, before seven o'clock. An old, experienced woman, the *materyot*—she has done it hundreds of times already—approaches the girl who is croaching on the ground with her legs outspread; the fringe apron has been drawn up and now covers the virgin breasts. In a glowing chamber-pot (*rokyet*) is a glowing coal. The woman blows on it, then takes hold of the pot with two succulent pieces of wood (*ketit*) of the sacred *Erythrina tomentosa*, places the glowing coal on a wooden, spoon-like instrument and applies it to the swollen clitoris, which gradually chars. At this moment a shrill cry arises from the throats of the hundreds of women present as a sign that the operation has been gone through without a moan. A powder is now spread on the wound. The women, her nearest relatives and the guests of honor, fetch garlands of a clinging plant (*Ficus sp.*) resembling asparagus and hang them around the girl. Then the girl retires; she is withdrawn from public life for four months and is called *tarusyot,* the newly-circumcised. But the guests dance on, all day long. Soon the external splendor of the *tarusyot* is returned, the thigh-bells and a *goysit.* Six of the little girls cast themselves upon the bells and at once they are tied around their slim thighs. Now the stamping begins in real earnest: the girls by themselves with their song "Eyo leyo leyo la," the *morans* and *layoni* by themselves going through mad saltations with their flowing manes.

. . . and the novice, the newly-circumcised, remains in the hut with a good aunt, cared for by her and other women, who mutually relieve one another as nurses. Only little children have free entrance there. They bring milk and entertain the poor girl.

Driven by curiosity, I cross the threshold of the sanctuary in spite of all the precepts of etiquette, at a moment when no woman is in the hut. I peer into the darkness of the interior. On the floor near the entrance the girl is crouching among children, looks at me disconcertedly, and instantly covers her head with a cow-hide. Ashamed at my obtrusiveness, I withdraw. Soon one of the women appears and asks me in a dignified manner whether I have seen the *tarusyot.* She implores me to spit on her hand. Were I to refuse the circumcised girl would start a hunger strike and die: all because I have seen her. But my spittle, with which the forehead of the girl would be smeared, would rectify everything. The wish of the suppliant woman is complied with; I give her a tip in addition. She disappears into the hut, but soon returns rubbing her hands with cow-dung, the Nandi soap.

Now the girl begins a secluded life, as if in a nunnery. First she puts on a tightly fitting, girdled leather dress (*nyargit*), topped with a large three-cornered cowl (*soynet*). In the cowl there are two peep-holes, which are sometimes bordered with beads; she may leave her neck and mouth free. Besides the usual neck rings, straw-colored (*malingotyet*) or dark brown stalks (*malusyet*) may be wound around her neck. Together with her ordinary brass or iron spirals, others woven of bast strips (*siringwet*) are wound around the wrists of the novice, and on her upper arm small pieces of straw are wound, like a long string of beads. In her hand she holds a little staff (*mutuolik*) of four rods bound together.

She speaks in a low voice, and does not touch her food or other objects with her hands, but with small, wooden sticks. If she were to touch food with her hands "her future husband would die." She does not call people but beats her leather dress with her staff, her *mutuolik*. She speaks little, does not spit on the ground, as is the custom of her parents, but on her hand. Usually the visier of the cowl is open, but if a man approaches her, she lets it down over her face. She does not sleep in her mother's house, where she would meet her father too often, whom she anxiously avoids, but with some aunt or other woman. In the hut she lives in a clean doll's house (*soumot*), made for her from the plaster that the negroes prepare, and often painted on the outside with ornaments and figures. Her real abode is outside in a hedge near the hut. There

139

she plays, there her friends come to visit her. For pastime, she has built herself at the entrance to the enclosed hedge, a little obelisk-shaped tower (*kaptiryot*), looking like some fantastic termite structure. The foundation, with its hollow trestle of rods fastened together, her old *materyot* has made for her, but the plaster walls and the door of interlaced sticks the girl has made herself. The number of obelisks in such a hedge depends on the number of the circumcised who are sharing their lot in it. In this tower the round, cadmium yellow fruit of the nightshade (*solanum campylanthum,* the *labotyat*) is kept. The playground is surrounded by a low clay wall. There every afternoon the girls roll the nightshade balls and play a "cattle-game" with them, counting and regarding them as their herds of cattle. There is a little wooden trough on the ground at the entrance. In it red ochre is mixed with water, and the body, clothing and ornamentation is colored with it from time to time—it is a kind of vanity box. Before finally leaving the hut the girls embed the nightshade fruits in the plaster of the wall, giving it a very odd appearance.

Four free months are now spent by the *tarusyot* in this nunnery; she does not work at all, and so her body becomes fuller, which is what is wanted. The wound is healed, she has recovered. A concluding feast is then given which is celebrated very ceremoniously by the women of the district. On the last night no man may enter the hut in which all the guests sleep together. A remarkable procedure is carried out there. The oldest women of the village assume the offices of teachers. On the day before they led the *tarusyot* to the forest and taught her the healing power of different herbs. Then they return to her hut

140

where beer is ready for the women. On the way friends give her all sorts of rules of life. "You are not a girl any more now, you are a grown person. If you meet a man, step out of his way to the left." Another experienced matron says to her, "Do not sleep with other men when your husband is aware of it." "When your husband has bought (married) you, you will receive a child (become pregnant), then you should not stand, but sit." And the like. Late in the evening the *materyot* goes into the forest with four or five women to seek a lion. She has previously been following its tracks, and places the earth, in which its claws are imprinted, in her leather cloak. Now a jug of beer is offered the lion. The old women stroke it until it becomes tame and begins to lick their hands. Then it is bound and at night brought to the hut of the circumcised girl, where it is tied to the main post of the house. The girls, who can hardly distinguish the contours of the beast of prey in the dark, are so frightened that they urinate. Now they must eat all the insects off the lion, then the lion urinates, and its urine is sipped up by all the newly-circumcised girls, who have still been unable to recover from their fright. Only then do the old women lead the lion back to its lair in the forest. The girls must eat still other such repulsive delicacies. Women bring them fleas and lice in the leather of their clothing; they also lick clean a ring dipped in the mucous of the vagina.

The circumcised girls believe in the authenticity of the lion in full seriousness. When I tried to imply that the lion was a disguised woman roaring into a pot, the *tarusyots* almost wept because of the dirty lie I was telling about their grand experience. I consequently had to desist from further explanations.

141

On the final day, the next morning, the *morans* come together at some distance from the women, who have been watching all night, while the *old men* go to visit the women's house courteously to greet the old women and the *tarusyot*. They hold grass in their hands and extend it to the *tarusyot* as a sign of greeting. Outside in front of the hut there is beer in a large receptacle. The women sipping the beer can not be seen because round about them others, magnificently attired, are performing a beer dance. Pressed close to each other, the married women of various years move along, beating the leather parts of the coats and thus giving a clapping accompaniment to their song. The dance is concluded by the *tarusyots*, who, in honor of this festive occasion, have painted themselves a very deep red with iron oxide earth.

The cauterization instead of the circumcision of men and women occurs only among the Nandi and the related Nyangori. And not among all of these either. The closely related Lumbwa circumcise their girls with a thin, sharp knife (*mwatindet*), which is also used by many of the Nandi. In this case, the excised clitoris is placed in cow-manure and then buried in the cow stall. Among many Nandi circumcision is said to be performed first with a knife and then for disinfection and stanching of the blood the burning iron as described above is used. The practical performance of this operation is even more difficult to visualize than that of mere cauterization, for which reason this version sounds quite unlikely.

Even among the related Sebeyi, who have more Bantu blood in them, the girls, as among all other shepherd peoples, are circumcised and not cauterized. On the morning it is to take place, the girl winds a string of cowrie-shells around her head and lies down on the ground with her hands under her head. On her breast is a cow-bell, originally, no doubt, to prevent her running away. The assistant holds her head as the circumcisor sits down in front of her. Everyone watches how the old woman severs the clitoris with a stroke of the knife. Now the girl receives some bread and porridge from her mother, which she immediately spits out.*

Among the Elkoyni, circumcision is performed in a similar manner, in the presence of the masculine sex.

---

* The period of convalescence is the same as that of the boys.

77. Nandi Cosmetics

COURTSHIP

Among the Elkoyni it is the father who goes courting for his son. Right after the convalescence of the young man his father goes looking for the bride of whom his son has often spoken to him. The father of the girl may live far away. Much preparation is made and the course of things in general is very slow. "First give me tobacco," says the old man as a sign of his accommodating attitude. The next day the father gives the old man the desired smoking tobacco, which he immediately begins to chew. Now comes the main question: the size of the dowry demanded. "Three cows, two goats," is the answer. The father returns home again, goes to the old man the next day with two *morans*, who drive two cows in front of them. He leaves the goats at home. "Where are the goats?" are the first words with which the daughter greets her future father-in-law. "The goats are at home, drinking beer," the latter simpers. The next morning the father and son, the *moran*, take an ox and exchange it somewheres for a good deal of Eleusine corn. Then seven women and the mother of the young man fetch corn in the place of beasts of burden, while six others look for six large earthenware receptacles for the beer. When the beer has been brewed, the old man and his daughter are invited; they come at noon from their distant residence together with other old people. Over the beer a lively discussion is held about the marriage affairs. Then the drinking is continued, but the bridegroom does not drink: the beer was bought for his ox. All get drunk and do not go home until the next day. Both fathers, the daughter and the *moran* remain over the last pot to bring the matter to a close before noon. The next day the parents go with the two goats to the old man and are invited to dinner, whereupon they say, "My son will now fetch your daughter." "He may fetch her after three days." So lingeringly does everything proceed. On the stipulated day the bridegroom appears with four *morans*, conceals himself in the forest near the house and lies in waiting for his bride until she comes to fetch water. Then he seizes her and leads her home. She yells and weeps, "Leave me alone! Father! Mother! Come, the people are taking me away!" Sometimes she must be beaten, because she refuses to go.

Among the Sebeyi, if his bride will not have him, the groom seizes her with four or five friends wherever he meets her. She cries, "I do not want this person!" It may

145

come to a point where his friends hold her down while he has her.

Not always is the circumcised girl "still to be had." It often happens that the bride has already been wooed before circumcision, or has secretly engaged herself, even though this engagement has no binding validity since she is uncircumcised. Usually her father has bartered her away for a stipulated price to an old friend by promising him her hand while she is still young, without her knowledge and against her will. If the girl has a lover who is serious, he seduces her to have her circumcised.

Such a seduction is by no means to be considered as romantic and dramatic as is often the case among us. The very fact that the girl must absolutely be circumcised in order for her husband to be sure of his *property*, means that such a seduction cannot take place in secret. The circumcision takes place publicly at a dance festival, and then again the girl must rest afterwards for four months. The purpose, action, and place where the couple stay are therefore known to a large number of people.

When her mother is working in the field and her father is drinking, or when her parents are busy in some other way, the girl is fetched by her seducer. He has already made arrangements with an old woman in a neighboring village to have the circumcision take place there. Such a couple may be met in bright daylight. According to the custom of the negroes he goes ahead while she follows, without any baggage. The only thing to attract attention is that both are exceptionally well ornamented and painted. The ear-block of the girl is also set with beads, something unusual. They walk along seriously, like people *decided* upon an important deed. People that pass

146

around and whisper to each other, "That fellow has seduced her" (Nandi).

One early morning a widow, the mother of a seduced
girl, came shouting and crying to me to help her; yesterday, as she was making beer, the Nandi-*moran* Ar-ap
Metee had dragged away her little twelve year old daughter, Tavarandi, to be circumcised. The only way I could
help her was by pointing out the probable direction in
which the couple could have fled. The woman was inconsolable, as a bitch whose young had been drowned; she
swore she would set fire to the house of the *moran* and
set out on her search. Towards noon little Tavarandi
came back past my hut accompanied by a young woman
who had helped her in her flight. Everything was supposed to have been prepared. The thigh-bells and other
circumcision ornamentation had been collected, the old
circumcisor had also been fetched: but—at the last moment the seducer withdrew out of cowardice and fear,
and, in spite of all the provisions, had left everything in
the lurch. The Nandi who heard that, girls and boys as
well as adults, had only one thing to say, one judgment
to pass on the cowardly fellow, "He's no *moran*, he's a
woman!"

I know a case that was just the opposite. A father
wanted to marry off his daughter to an old fellow. The
day for the circumcision had already been decided upon.
But the girl succeeded in convincing her lover, a young
moran, that she be seduced and circumcised. They
had already fled, had collected all the circumcision
ornamentation, when the conscience of the daughter
awoke to the anger of her father, whom she greatly feared;
she turned right about face at the circumcision, her dis-

heartened friend followed her home. To this day their parents have no idea of what happened. But her lack of courage became fateful for her. Several days later she had to engage herself to the despised old man. Directly after the circumcision he became her lawful bridegroom, and as a sign of betrothal they exchanged bracelets of woven grass that are worn on the right arm. The fate of the young woman was thereby sealed. She now becomes the property of her wedded husband, and cannot legally marry anyone else. The grass is preserved until the breast-plates are donned, then a goat steps on it (Nandi).

A girl who has been circumcised is called among the Nandi *keleldet,* if, after the women's festival she has doffed her tightly fitting nun's dress and cowl and put on a regular leather dress. She now wears her brand new breast-plates (*taok*) and red and blue ear-blocks (*muita*), but now she has her new goat-leather mantle laced up in back, and not as later in front, and all her neck and breast ornamentation is now covered up. Only her head and a part of her neck, like a modern bust is visible out of the leather. A diadem of cowrie-shells borders her relatively long hair, rubbed in with red earth and fat, diagonally across her hair runs another strap to which usually boar tusks are sewed. Her back is made beautiful by a cow-bell hanging on a strap adorned with cowries from her girdle. The least movement will set the cow-bell ringing. In her hand the girl carries a foliated staff (*kirundut*), her arms and ankles are adorned with spirals of plaited bast (*siringuet*). The girl may thus be seen going about for days and weeks, longing for her salvation, waiting to be taken to her new home. Never alone, she must always have some one to accompany her, be it only a baby girl . . . Actually these *keleldet* must wear the prescribed dress until her bridegroom comes to take her away, but her parents often wish her to end her idleness. So she shaves her head, throws away the foliated staff, removes the cowrie ornamentation from her head, her cowrie girdle, the vegetable spirals and the cow-bell, shoves her mantle around to the front, and in the twinkling of an eye she is no longer a sexually dependent being. Now she may give herself to any man—even if her husband is yet to come to take her away—without being afraid of offending the ruling morality. A *keleldet* with unshaven head could never be seduced! It seems as if the shaving of hair has magically done away with everything impure and taboo in her previous existence.

I have followed the fate of four *keleldet* who were circumcised at the same time. They afford a deep insight into the sorrows of loving negro women.

The husband of the first was in jail, sentenced to four years for cow stealing. She loves him and waits for him with patient resignation. She was also the last of all four to have her head shaved and put aside her *keleldet* dress while her friends had long changed. Long, difficult years of temptation are now before her.

The husband of the second was a brute. She had hardly come into her new home, when her husband gave her so much work that she refused to do it. She received a sound thrashing and her husband ripped both lobes of her ears that were stretched out as thin as strings. So she left her husband, ran to her mother, got the lobes of her ears to grow together as well as she could, and became a prostitute.

The third, as appeared after the conclusion of her period, was pregnant. It must have had happened before circumcision, and with one that was uncircumcised too, with a *layoni*. Her husband, but who was not yet legally so, would not have her. Then her parents seriously thought of marrying her to one of the related Massai tribe, among whom pre-marital pregnancy was not degrading. But that was only talk. A man in the forties took her to himself for a short time to try her, where she helped in the household together with his legal wife. He intended to marry her later, on condition that she would choke the child. But he soon drove her away, for reasons unknown to me. At last an honest, if not handsome, negro took pity on her and finally married her.

Only the fourth will marry without any special intermezzo, if, as arranged, her husband, the father of my kitchen boy, comes to take her in a month. She has already shaved her head . . . the temptation for *vice* begins.

If parents have a circumcised daughter at home who is not yet engaged, it is not long before suitors appear from near and far. Courtship begins at once. Then the wooing *moran* may be seen going to the hut with a labiate flower peeping out of his toga at the upper arm, accompanied by his mother if he is not married, by his oldest (first) wife, if he is. He squats in front of the hut and waits patiently for hours. He is not quite alone, he meets rivals with similar purposes. He usually is discovered by her parents who do not want to be too hasty in such an important matter. He appears again the next morning with another flower and repeats the courting scene. The same thing may happen many times until the girl finally makes her choice. Naturally they had to agree first in regard to the size of the dowry. Usually two or three cows and five goats are enough (Nandi). The girl's father buys her some more ornamentation, such as iron spirals for her calves, then he goes with her and a little boy and girl to his son-in-law who is arranging a beer banquet. Only the old folks drink beer; the young woman gets milk. Then the father-in-law slaughters on ox which is consumed in the forest or in a little *men's house* especially built for this purpose, decorated with banana leaves; but the young woman eats no meat. She has drunk milk, and milk and meat may not be taken within twenty-four hours of each other.*

Only one person is missing, but she is not missed: the mother-in-law. She is taboo to her son-in-law and may not enter his home while he is there (Nandi).

Among the Kitosh the dowry consists of two cows, a ten shilling marriage fee for the sultan of the village, a cotton suit for the father-in-law and a spade for the mother-in-law. Among the Baganda the price is higher and may also be paid in cash. The prices are not set definitely. A father sometimes assesses his daughter above the usual standard; "she is new," he adds, meaning to say by that that she is still a virgin (Elkoyni).

Among the Kitosh it is the custom, as has been told me by many, that the suitor first makes advances to his future mother-in-law and secretly seduces her before he goes after the daughter. Only then does she recommend him to her husband and the young man may now successfully woo her daughter. The mother-in-law may not visit them until they have several children; even then she may not set her foot upon the inside of the hut near the

151

hearth, but sits near the door because she is afraid of her son-in-law.†

Among the negroes a mother-in-law is not tolerated in the new home.

---

* It is interesting to note that this precept, occurring in a similar form among the Jews, does not apply to blood drunk mixed with the milk. The reason given me for this was that blood and milk both came from the living animal.

† The black has one word for "to be afraid" and "to be ashamed" *"kopa"* (*Suaheli*).

78. Family Life

DEFLORATION AND COITUS

The young husband says at night, "Spread out the cow-hide."* Whereupon the young woman, in obedience to his will, spreads out the cow-hide, the mattress of the shepherd peoples, on the ground. The *moran* lies down on it while his wife makes her own bed some few feet away. "Come!" calls the shy husband. She comes, but not with steady step, half afraid, half ashamed. "What's the matter? Come!" he says. She is silent. He seizes her by the hand, embraces her and grasps her breasts. "Let

---

* A bridegroom or husband will never mention the name of his bride or wife. There is a spell over it.

me alone!" she moans gently, but more out of passive passion than fear. Intertwined in hot embrace, they sleep together. "Then," a reliable married man told me, "she is vexed because I hurt her so that blood came. The next morning the *moran* goes to the river to bathe. In the evening at eight o'clock the same thing takes place. But now twice. He likes hers and she his, so she does not resist at all this night. The next day another man has her in the forest and gives her ten shillings for cohabitation. If she cries out the result is a great scandal" (Elkoyni).

Among the Nandi, in case his wife should offer any resistance during the nuptial night, the young husband's friends wait outside to hold her down. If it is difficult to deflower her, the husband takes a knife and cuts her hymen without her knowledge what he is going to do. She moans, weeps, cries that all can hear her, "I am dying, I am dying! It is all my father's fault, because he wants more cattle!" The angry husband answers, "I must give your father a cow tomorrow, so I must first take away your virginity." Sometimes eleven or twelve days pass before the *moran* succeeds in deflowering her.

Virginity among the Nandi is not very highly prized, perhaps that is why promiscuity is rampant among the black girls before circmcision. I have even heard from them, as well as from the Bagishu, that they preferred girls that were not virgins for the reason that cohabitation with them was easier. They therefore shut one eye if young fellows take care of this matter for them in their uncircumcised sweethearts.

In spite of the disregard of virginity there prevails among the Nandi a natural modesty that manifests itself in certain forms of shame. For instance, this is the way

154

a young married couple behave in bed. It is evening. They have lain down to sleep on their cow-hides; he is on one, she on another, according to the custom. They are separated by a clay elevation, like a low wall. The husband does not want to sleep, she does not want to either. They want each other. But he does not come to her, nor will she go to him. The negress must also be begged. Then he clears his throat, "Hm, hm," to make known his erotic readiness, his desire. He, the proud *moran*, clears his throat only once. But, this is sufficient to cause her to get up from her bed, turn her head away from him, draw her already protruding lips together into a sulking mien, shrug her shoulders and let out a very low, a half whispering, half whining, high-pitched "e-e-eh-e-e-h"— like an ape that has been disturbed—as if to say, "Let me alone . . . I am tired, want to sleep," or something like that.

In this gesture there is tragedy and comedy, naturalness and acting, innocence and sophistication, resignation and self-consciousness, modest coyness and hot spirited calculation, play and seriousness, a whole drama is symbolized: a drama of feminine inferiority and attachment physiologically, but superiority and vanity psychically.

Kisses are rare ,but less so among the young than among the old. They are moist and audible. Licking is unknown to the negress as is sucking of the breasts to the negro. There is no biting either.

The lateral position is the usual one for coitus among the Nandi and many other shepherd peoples. That prostitutes command all twenty-four erotic figures, including *cunnilingus* and other *raffinements,* does not disprove it. They have learned that from the Europeans, Arabs, Indians and Suaheli.* The Suaheli especially set the fashion here. They have spread among the women even outside their sphere of influence a grinding motion in coitus, the so-called *titikisha*. The other negro women have apparently learned from them also how to tickle their husbands under the arm-pits in order to arouse them (Baganda). But we shall remain with the Nandi. The man sometimes touches the down on the *mount of Venus* to excite himself, but never the vagina. On the other hand, the woman never touches the membrum, except to clean it at the end of the act with a cloth, the loincloth already mentioned, or, in lack of this, with leaves. Perhaps they have also learned this concluding bit of etiquette from the Suaheli? But the black woman feels no disgust at semen. In every other case the blacks feel that touching the sexual parts with the fingers is something impure, obnoxious, loathesome. "How can he then touch food with those same fingers?"† That is the objection they raise against it. It is probably due to this disgust that the Nandi never takes his penis in his hand when urinating, but performs this act like a woman in a crouching position, like the colored Mohammedans (*e.g.*, Somali) otherwise he would dirty his clothes.

Because of the disgust they feel at touching the genitals, which they so obviously manifest, it can be seen that the negroes are not taken over by any *raffinements* or perversities in their usual sexual life. As a matter of fact, the negress, especially the Semi-hamite (Nandi) is the most normal woman in the world. We must fundamen-

---

* According to information of my guarantor Baurat A .... the Wasuaheli prefer noon time for coitus, "it is then healthy and very fruitful."

† They have neither spoons nor forks, but eat with their hands.

tally revise our conception of the moral depravity of negroes, based on absolutely false knowledge, when we see how sensitive they are even against indecent words or gestures. How modest are their emotions in spite of, or rather because of their incarnate idea *"naturalia non sunt turpia!"* A Nandi woman, even a harlot, greets a *moran* with graceful shyness, turning her head aside modestly as she extends her hand to him, as if she were afraid to look into his eyes. In the presence of older people no *moran* would dare to make his wife or a girl a proposal, or attempt to embrace her. The slightest suggestive gesture is prohibited. No indecent word may be let fall in the presence of older people. I was a witness when a harlot in the presence of elders told an incident and used a harmless word,* but was sneered at for her, impudent rudeness. Euphemistic phrases are rather resorted to. If a woman had her menstruation, she says, for example, she was wounded by the neighboring Kavirondo.

The negro woman has nothing to do with perversities, they have no appeal to her, she finds no pleasure in them. If there is an exceptional case of perversity, it has certainly been learned from the European or Arab. She finds pleasure only in normal coitus: she has not yet placed her tongue and mouth in the service of the erotic, and she neither likes nor allows a man to substitute any thing for his sexual parts. In answer to the question, why she did not like it, a Baganda girl answered with naive candor, "The dear Lord has made the mouth for eating, the *vulva* for coitus." Though a prudish European woman could never bring herself to utter such words, it would not pre-

---

* She told how an Englishman had had an affair with a Nandi woman for some time, but in a fit of anger shot her; the bullet hit her in the buttocks.

vent her from desiring such perversities. And in spite of such obscene words, she could hardly reach such a moral height of genuine modesty as found among negroes.

That the masculine youth like to discuss erotic matters among themselves does not contradict my contention that the blacks, in their manner of thinking, their erotic deeds and actions, are more moral than we are. They conceive the sexual as being beyond the moral.

I once listened to a conversation of my boys from my tent as they sat around the camp fire, and heard nothing that really could be called bad. The one topic under discussion, to be sure, was that of coitus. Two tribes were represented: of the Bantu the Bagishu, of the Semi-hamites the Sebeyi. The one were telling that they cohabited only in a lateral position, the others that they did it one upon the other. Both were maintaining that their way of cohabiting was the better. The Bagishu said further that their wives got no children if they cohabited with many men (*tomba*). Venereal diseases were also thought to cause sterility among women. In the nearby town of Kitale there were negro prostitutes; the negroes had to pay two shillings for a visit. All this I have taken down in my journal word for word, just as I give it. These rather informative remarks can hardly be called obscene. They are harmless compared to our smutty jokes.

Naturally not every negro tribe is to be considered the same. A line must also be drawn between those that have come in contact with the European, and those not yet *blessed with culture*. The Bantu at any rate are much looser than the Semi-hamite shepherd peoples.

At Mpolegoma (Uganda) I heard boys of the Bnioli

tribe beating their hands rhythmically and calling after
the passing girls or women:

Niapala, niapala pehumunie,
Moyo humunie omnie heshillingi.

(My heart longs for a vagina,
Give me vagina and shilling!)

The girls are bothered little by the natural frivolity of
such young scamps. A Nandi would be ashamed to tease
the women so openly and aggressively with indecent chat-
ter as those Bantu did. He may, of course, discuss natural
things and use strong words, but never purely out of
pleasure for what is indecent, but simply because the
natural is not indecent to him. For instance, a *moran*
may come to his girl and, make fun of his wife by telling
that she had continually farted during coitus. And both
laugh at it like children.

The fact also that it sometimes happens that a Nandi
couple cohabit in a hut in which there are other people
(only!) of the same age, does not invalidate my contention: at night a negro hut is wrapped in Egyptian darkness; nothing can be seen. And certainly no one would
remain awake to listen as would happen in such cases with
us. It is simply not bothered about.

If a smutty joke is told, its contents must be of a didac-
tic nature, it must have a moral. I give a story told me by
a young woman:

An Ndorobbo* had a very beautiful daughter. As his
wife began to grow old, he thought of how he could sleep
with his daughter. He therefore did not have her circumcised, or she would get married. His wife kept urging
that the girl be circumcised, but the old man always had

---

* A tribe of wild men related to the Nandi.

159

an evasive answer. Since the Ndorobbo have no cattle, but live only on wild animals, he went hunting, shot a buck, ate a part of it and hung the rest up on a tree. When he returned home his wife asked him about the hunt. The porridge was ready (which is really to be eaten with meat or milk). "God has given me no luck," was the answer. The next day he went hunting again. Again he killed a buck, ate a piece of it, hung the rest up on a tree, returned home to his wife, who again asked about his luck, but to whom he answered, "God has granted me no luck." Their young daughter had almost no food. The Ndorobbo repeated this act ten days in succession. Since the little one was almost starved, the woman said to her husband, "Go to the soothsayer and ask him what is to be done that you may capture game!" The man went away, made believe he had been to the soothsayer, returned and said to his wife, "The soothsayer said that I am to sleep with my daughter." His wife answered, "Good, let it take place." She now left the hut and went to a neighbor while her husband slept with her daughter at home. The next day the elders of the village visited him. He was muttering quite unintelligently, "It is the same, it is the same!" When his wife came home the old man said to her, "I thought God was wise, but hers is just the same as yours."

It is interesting to note that in this story the despised* Ndorobbo are made the actors, because even in a story the Nandi will not accept the possibility of incest in his own tribe.

The blacks take cognizance of degrees of kinship with painstaking exactitude in matters of sex. Incest is abso-

* They would not shift the story to a very hostile tribe, like the Kavirondo, because they hate them so much that they do not want to learn any good from them.

lutely out of the question. Even cousins would not have sexual intercourse with each other, let alone marry. Many a European, who is proud of his morality, could take an example from the *immoral* black. Grown up brothers and sisters never sleep in the same room. Even when blood brotherhood has been concluded marriage or cohabitation is out of the question. It is moving to see in what a tactful and well-bred manner such "brothers and sisters" behave. Even an allusion to something indecent must not be made in their presence, whether it refers to them or not. "Quiet! Why, here is my sister (brother)!" is what one hears, if the conversation is turned to something lascivious.

Blood brotherhood is considered to be just as genuine as uterine blood relationship. The two members act exactly as brothers and sisters do. "We have both been born of one belly," such a couple repeatedly assured me.

If two people who are attracted to each other by pure friendship wish to conclude brotherhood, the man and not the girl first proposes it with the words, "I want to have a sister now." She agrees. In the presence of many others they mutually cut a small wound in the palm of their righ hand, near the thumb, and suck each other's blood. They have then become brother and sister "as of one belly." Now they must always stand by each other in all matters, the brother must protect his sister. Valuable gifts are mutually exchanged. Even prostitutes behave tenderly, modestly and with consideration towards such blood brothers. I repeat, coitus between them is out of the question, it would be like incest. Such blood brotherhood can take place only between members of two different tribes, *e.g.*, the Kikuyu and the Nandi.

The Nandi's abhorrence of incestuous cohabitation may

161

also be seen from the curses he uses. *"Ikum kaumet"* ("———your mother") is the most terrible curse a Nandi can utter. It is equalled in coarseness by *"Ikum tain"* (———your cow"), and is to be looked upon not so much as a sign of the Nandi's abhorrence of sodomitic acts, as rather of the sacred veneration he feels towards cattle, which are placed on a par with women.

For in the imagination of the negro the animal plays a human part. In his marvelous fables, animals appear as human beings. Not humanized as in Aesop, no, they are human beings. And since all nature revolves about the sexual, by which it is dominated, it is understandable that Eros is made the bearer of many phenomena that for us have no meaning, but for the negro are brought into close contact with his sexual life. Who would interpret the constant nightly wail of the goat-owl (*wuarire*) as the Nandi does? In its call the negro hears the word *Takirorunge, i.e.,* "Stick it (the membrum) in." That is why a Nandi woman when strolling with a *moran* feels her modesty somewhat injured if she hears the call.

According to Hollis the calls of the male and female owls are also interpreted erotically. The male says:

Ti-pchu, opwa o-ngephe sukus tukul,

Come girls, let us all go and urinate.

whereupon the female answers:

Ke-le ne? Kipte-pirit tingwe!

What were you saying? Your member is like a rope!

but the male retorts:

Ke-le ne? chep-te-kuset ipero!

What were you saying? Your pudendum is like a bunch of tobacco leaves.

162

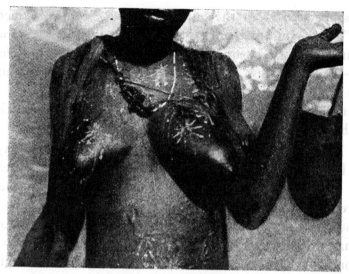

79. Decorated Breasts

MENSTRUATION

The age at which menstruation begins among the Nandi girls cannot be determined since the natives as a rule have no idea how old they are. One must guess at the age, as many ethnographers do, which is nothing but guesswork and therefore of only casual reliability. As a rule the girls have their first menstrual period between their twelfth and thirteenth years. It is not told to parents and sisters, but only to friends.

A menstruating woman is everywhere considered unclean, the negro says *dirty*. She may not cook; she does not extend her hand to a *moran* in greeting, whereby she tactfully makes known to him her *dirty condition*. Nor may she be asked to cohabit. If she has inadvertently given him her hand, and then explains to him at night that she is bleeding, a quarrel may arise. The negro does not touch a menstruating woman. But the woman, by giving him her hand has misled him, allowing him to think that she was not in an *unclean* condition, has consequently led him to believe, on false representations, that she would have no objection to coitus. It often happens that a negress, in order to get rid of an obtrusive person, will simply lie about her condition. She says, "I am ill."

Like every woman, she is in a condition of high erotic excitement during her menstrual period and longs for sensual pleasure more than usually. The medicinemen, who have a deep understanding of the feminine *psyche*, readily make use of this erotic tension for their own pleasure. Girls and women willingly give themselves to them during the period; they give themselves without compunction (Nandi). It is also known to women that they are particularly apt to be impregnated at this time; and so women who long for motherhood run after men, especially the medicinemen.

She may be seen at this time wearing dirty clothes, and the desiccated blood stains leave no doubt as to the reason for her carelessness. If blood falls on the hide on which she sleeps, it is washed away the next day with cow urine. The woman goes to the cow, strokes it on the back of the neck with gentle blows until it begins to urinate. She receives the liquid into her calabash and washes the hide clean with it. Among the Bagishu women I noticed that, presumably to stanch the blood, at any rate, to receive it, they place green leaves (probably of the *Emilia integrifolia*) about and in the sexual parts.

164

The disgust a man feels at the blood of menstruation may be seen from an incident which my neighbor experienced. The latter gave his sleeping sack, which was stained with blood, to his two boys to wash. Both stubbornly refused to do it. No threats, no promised tips could change their minds. Since no feminine help could be obtained, an old man was finally brought round to wash it for a relatively high remuneration. Out of the same disgust most negro tribes eat no zebra meat. "*Kuma sawasawa mtu*" ("The vagina of the zebra is just like that of a human being").

At the end of the period, which lasts three days at the most, the negress takes a good bath in cold water.

80. Virgin Girl

81. Pregnant Kitosh
Woman

PREGNANCY

Pregnancy, like the monthly condition, is also considered unclean. A man prefers not to sleep with his wife the first night after conception. In this case the *ejaculatio seminis* is external (*coitus interruptus*). If this did not happen the child would be "brought to shame" in its mother's body. Among the Sebeyi it is believed that the child would have a white eruption. For this reason a pregnant woman does not give herself to any one. A dressed Nandi woman, who appeared to be pregnant, immediate-

166

ly removed her blouse and uncovered her breasts, when asked about her condition, in order that the men might see from their flabbiness that she was not pregnant. If the child in her womb is three months old, the mother's period of seclusion begins. Among the Nandi she throws a shabby piece of goat-skin about her shoulders, and now every one knows: she is pregnant. Her husband does not bother much about her, and satisfies his desire with other women; and considering his usual polygamous bent, it is no wonder that, in view of the enforced abstention from all sexual intercourse with his wife until after the child is born, be takes a second wife.

. . . in the meantime the germ in the womb grows and matures. It soon becomes evident to the neighborhood, who give a dance of joy in honor of the pregnant woman. The nearer the day of birth approaches, the greater becomes the woman's anxiety of the delivery. A kind of beer fete is now held for the exorcism of demons.

First, two old men and then two *morans* one after the other besprinkle the interior of the hut with beer. The consecrator holds in one hand the cow tail that is indispensible at a drinking fete—the scepter of the host or of the guests singing beer songs—in the other the small calabash (*muendet*), with holes in its sides, filled with bear and serving as a ladle; the one as a symbol of cattle, the other of beneficial grain. Amid prayers or religious incantations, one after the other, they pour beer out of the ladle, first around the beer pot, then on the ground in all corners of the hut, sometimes one takes a sip from the spoon in order to besprinkle, as with a vaporizer, the spot where beer is to be poured out. The chorus of the beer fete answers from time to time an amen-like utterance.

This religious prelude to the feast of pregnancy also takes place at other feasts. It is only now that the real fete begins. Both wives of the master of the house, one of whom is visibly pregnant, are called to the beer pot together with the mother of the blessed woman. They hold their open hands one above the other, like windows of a house. An old man then pours beer, in the manner described, into the topmost hand, and it gradually runs down into the lowest one. Then the pouring of beer ceases and the three women sip up the soup like beverage from their not particularly clean hands. Then they return to their place, disappearing in the background. Now a happy delivery may be looked forward to (Nandi).

Childbirth sometimes occurs outside, but usually within the hut. The suffering woman sits on a low stone. Three women help her. One of them, standing behind her, massages her back and at delivery holds her mouth and nose with her hand to stop her breath or the little one would die; the other two hold her legs. Then the child is drawn out by the head. The umbilical cord is severed with a knife and the placenta buried in cow-dung. In the case of a small vagina a knife is used at delivery; the vagina is then cut through to the perineum. The midwife kisses the new-born child and thus blows her life breath and spittle through its mouth and nose. The child is then washed with cold water. If the child cries or makes any sound before complete delivery (?), "the mother and all previous children will die" (Nandi).

If a married woman bears a child that is due to illegitimate cohabitation, she must reveal the name of its real father to the midwife "or the child would otherwise die" (Baganda). Among the Nandi a man refuses, as is the

168

custom, to pour milk out of a calabash onto the floor of
the hut if he suspects that his wife's delivery is due to
adultry. If she says to him, "Sir, I have slept with another man," he is silent and then answers, "If you have
slept with someone else, the child dies." Then he pours
out the milk.

It thus becomes understandable that the deceived husband, the slave of anger, finally throttles the "evil brood."

82. Gifts in Honor of
Birth of Twins

I was witness at a trial in which a *moran* was accused of
attempted infanticide, when he learned that his wife's
children were not his. It was certain that he had mis-
treated his wife (Nandi). Public opinion does not allow
an illegitimate child into the community, not so much
because it comes of a young mother who has not yet
publicly been declared mature, and is therefore considered
unclean, but rather because the demonic thought of *"pater*

semper incertus" presses like an incubus upon the patriarchal system, and a husband whose wife has borne him an illegitimate child cannot bear a living reminder of the shame suffered, making ridiculous the institution of marriage resting on the idea of private property.

Three, at the most four days are spent by the con-

83. Carrying of Infant

fined woman in *bed*, on the cow-hide, her couch. During this time she may touch nothing with her hand. She takes hold only of the calabash of milk, and not as usually, at its neck, but at the bottom. The woman is unclean and does not wash during these days. When the four days are passed she fetches cow-urine in a calabash that is stop-

170

ped with grass and with its washes the head of the child and her genitals. Only after the passage of three more days does the young mother go into the forest where she bathes in cold water. The only thing noteworthy in the diet of the confined woman is that she does not eat meat of fallen cattle, usually a favorite at other times.

For a whole month the father does not look at the little one, which at first is quite light in color, almost like a child of the Mediterranean race, "otherwise it would die." He does not enter his hut through the main door, but through the door for goats at the back. For a whole month likewise his wife may not cook for him. For sexual intercourse she is considered unclean for a much longer time, from four to six months (Nandi).

Among the Banganda the parturient woman rests on her knees between two posts or poles, holding tight with her hands, while the midwife lifts her breasts and tries to press the child out by massaging. The umbilical cord is cut off with a piece of sharp reed. The child is washed in cold water. During the seven days of confinement the midwife washes the child and takes care of the more important matters of the household.

Among the Bagishu also the women bring forth their children in a kneeling posture. The umbilical cord, severed with a knife, is tied off with banana bast. The woman after child birth bathes on the fourth day in warm water. After three months she has sexual intercourse with her husband, but the *ejaculatio seminis* is external. In general her husband is very tender towards her, and when first seeing her again he greets her with the words, "Thanks very much now you have given me a child."

As a sign of motherhood among the Nandi the women

171

wear a special leather neck band, formed of cowrie-shells, the *samwet*.

On the third day the new born child is viewed by the women, who bring all kinds of presents for him, especially ornaments. It is a general custom, at the showing of the child, to present it later with pieces of money.

The coming of twins into the world is a cause for great joy. Then the whole village is excited. The people actually emulate each other in liberality. Even greater than the joy at their birth is the sorrow if both little ones happen to die. The inconsolable mother paints her distended breasts with clay (Kitosh).

The name of a child depends upon the events accompanying its birth. Thus, *Kyepsaa* means "Born in the open" and *Kyepkorr* "Born in the early morning" (Nandi).

84. Mother and Child

CARE OF CHILDREN

The mortality of infants is quite high because they are neglected; their care is confined simply to washing with cold water the inflammations of the groins. Usually the child is lugged about naked on its mother's back stuck in a loose cow-hide. If it dirties its mother with urine, the latter does not bother about it. She laughs at you if you remonstrate with her about it. The children are always bothered with phlegm due to the rapid changes in temperature between the heat of noon and the cold of

173

evening to which one is always exposed on the high plateau of Equatorial Africa. And the children go about entirely naked. There is no statistics on the mortality of children, but it can be concluded from the general use

85. Kitosh Mother

of the amulet against death, the *sepetaik* and the *songonyet*, that it is very high among the Nandi.

Before feeding the baby the mother washes the nipples of her breasts with water which she takes up in the palms of her hands, if she happens to have it near her.

While feeding her baby a woman is considered unclean. If she is cooking and wishes to feed her child at the same time, she must not touch the little one with her hands under any conditions or her husband would beat her to death. A girl brings the child to her breast and holds it while the mother sits on the ground supporting herself with two sticks (Nandi).

The breast is given the child until it has learned to speak, that is, until about the end of the second year.

86. Mother in Mourning

Later it drinks cow milk from the mother's hands (Nandi, Sebeyi).

Since the child often keeps its mother too busy because of the constant care and supervision that it requires, and she consequently, but involuntarily, neglects the erotic and forces it to the background, there are many cruel fathers who will not have their children in their huts, so that they are brought up by relatives, usually their grandmother. The mother visits her child now and then. The infant, very early weaned from mother's milk, is entirely under the care of its grandmother, who daily gives it her empty breasts to suck—a substitute for a teething ring or rubber nipple. From this fact there has arisen in anthropological literature the ever recurring, false picture of the suckling grandmother. Especially the erotic medicinemen do not tolerate their children at home because they are a hindrance to the sexual relations of their mother and father (Nandi).

The little negro children are charming, especially when their noses are clean; they do not cry often and their large deep eyes look intelligent. They are seldom punished because they are well behaved. Their older brothers and sisters play with them; even five year old children are seen carrying smaller ones around. They are carried either on the back, in their leather dress, like their mother does, or on the side, riding on the hip. The latter position is the usual one for many tribes (Kavirondo). If the child, carried in a knapsack by an older sister, cries for hunger, or any reason, the latter gently shakes the sack with both hands bent back, and the child falls asleep, rocked as if in a cradle.

The possession of children is considered a blessing among the negroes while bareness is a disgrace. Abortion is practiced only by prostitutes and sometimes by uncircumcised girls. The prostitutes practice it because a child is inconvenient in their trade. They obtain the abortive medicine from old women or medicinemen, and often have to pay a very high price for it. A Massai woman who already had a grown daughter but was herself a harlot informed me that a woman had given her an excellent medicine for the price of a hundred (?) shillings. This decoction (*sky-omeryat*) was taken only once, and then "for the rest of your life one did not get any children." If one did want a child, an antidote must be taken. A farmer who had much intercourse with uncircumcised girls, however, ex-

87. Nandi Woman
and Child

pressed himself very negatively on the efficacy of these means for abortion proffered by medicinemen. The thorough washing of the vagina after coitus probably serves the purpose attributed to these medicaments.

The negress is a fruitful being, bearing five children on the average. But I know mothers who had over twenty

177

children, of which, however, the greater part died. It is
difficult to determine whether more boys are born than
girls. At any rate the view common among the farmers
that the negroes prefer daughters to sons because the

88. Kavirondo Idyll

former represent capital in their dowry customs is untrue.
The mothers long especially for sons. Besides the fact
that this is natural to motherhood, the system of inheritance is such that the son or sons inherit everything at
the death of the father, while the daughters receive nothing. Why is this? Among the negroes there are no old
maids. And the father does not think of providing for his
son-in-law while he is still alive. But the mother finds a
support in her grown son (Nandi).

The father does not like his daughter if she has no children. If she has been married five years already and still has no children, one of her brothers or sisters appears one day and says, "I am now taking my sister to her mother because she has no children." At home her mother prepares a medicine for her, dissolved in cold water, which she takes three times a day. After a three-day cure she returns to her husband. These three days seem to have been devoted to extra-matrimonial life. According to information of negroes, if a woman among the Kavirondo, Nandi and Massai is childless after being married for some time, she takes the brother of her husband, who impregnates her. The latter comes to the hut of his brother. In front of it he has stuck his spear into the ground, according to the custom of *morans*. The brother now sees the spear and does not seem to bother about the matter any more.

89. Nandi Widow

WIDOWHOOD AND PROSTITUTION

The widow, be she childless or not, automatically becomes the property of her oldest brother-in-law, *i.e.*, the brother of her husband.

At the death of her husband, mourning and wailing, begins. Among many tribes she weeps* for some months, among many others only a short time. The doleful wailing is heart rending. It is a monotonous chanting by which she makes known to the world, as she sits in front of her hut from early morning to late at night:

"My lord is dead!"

---

* Otherwise the negress never weeps.

Other women also, especially her sisters, stand by her and accompany her in this dirge. One almost thinks that she fasts the whole time and sings her throat hoarse. Then the wailing ceases, she has ceased to be a widow; the brother of her deceased husband has taken her to himself. The dead man is seemingly externally forgotten (Bagishu).

Among the Nandi the bereft woman weeps for three days after the death of her husband. Then as a sign of mourning she shaves her head. She remains at home ten days; other women cook for her. Like a newly circumcised girl she touches nothing with her hands but with pieces of wood. After this short period of mourning she gives her neighbors beer and slaughters an ox, which is eaten by the friends of her husband. If she has small children or none at all, the oldest brother of the deceased takes her as his wife. If her brother-in-law is too young, she has intercourse, if she cares to, with other men, until her brother-in-law becomes of age, *i.e.*, circumcised. He builds her a hut where he sees fit, she rubs her head in with cow fat; for the second time she has ceased to be common property. I know a case in which a widow with a small child was *inherited* by her brother-in-law, a marriageable youth. But since he was still uncircumcised, he could not as yet take her to himself. But the sultan of the village granted him permission to be circumcised before the prescribed time, which is very unusual, since among the Nandi, as among other Massaioid shepherd peoples, the time for circumcision is definitely set, and may take place only every four and one-half years. He would have had to wait another year, but he was made an exception of, in order that he might marry immediately (Nandi).

181

The widow who has been taken into the house of her brother-in-law is not really to be considered as his wife, but rather his concubine. The very fact that the man does not have to give a dowry for her, does not have to *buy* her directly from her father, shows obviously that she is not considered his legitimate wife in the legal understanding of the negro. Moreover, it is not his duty to take her into his home. Deprived of her fine feminine ornamentation, foregoing the highest thing that a woman strives for, such a homeless woman is a sad picture of social loneliness, and everyone may take her for a night.

If the widow has a grown son, a *moran,* she does not remove her breast-plates, she enjoys the support of her son, is respected everywhere, and may even take part in beer parties as a matron.

The widower does not usually marry until a year after the death of his wife.

The condition that the widow at the death of her husband becomes a slave to her brother-in-law is naturally combatted by the missionaries. The newly converted widows therefore do not go to their brothers-in-law at the death of their husbands, and the missionary sees to it that they receive some means of livelihood. In a case known to me, a Christianized widow devoted herself entirely to pottery. In other instances the missionary is also placed in a dilemma, when, for instance, a woman in a negro harem wishes to become Christian. The Church has never condoned polygamy, and so she is not taken into the Christian community, even though the welfare of baptism is not denied her. On the other hand, a Christian negress who has married a non-convert, and thus contributes to the enlarging of his harem is expelled from the Protestant Church.

As suggested above, among the negroes, the widow represents the transition from wife to prostitute. Most of the concubines are recruited from among widows and recalcitrant wives, who for some reason or other have run away from their husbands. Since divorce for a woman once married—at least among the Nandi and related tribes —theoretically does not exist, since a woman may only marry once *legally*, after leaving her husband she can only play the part of a concubine to a new master. Even if, in her new home, she is placed on an equal footing with the legal wives, and takes part in domestic affairs, she enjoys no protection from the native authorities, and may without reason be driven out by her capricious master, and is looked upon in the neighborhood as a whore. And for all that she does not cost her husband a farthing! Every legitimate wife must be bought from her parents, but the concubine gives herself up without recompense. The bit of food that she receives from her husband can hardly be considered as pay for the work she does as a maid.

For the reason that the concubine is often introduced to whites as a *wife,* and sometimes wanders from man to man and from hand to hand, the European has spread abroad the false idea that marriage among the negroes is immoral, and that wives are exchanged. But one should not forget that to the negro concubine and prostitute are synonyms, and that in Europe such a relationship is usually also very loose; it is unjustified, to conclude from such a loose relationship that marriage in Europe is indecent.

The tribes investigated by me possess no word of their own for prostitute. They have generally taken it from the Suaheli. Among them *mlaya** means not only prostitute, an occupation fundamentally unknown to them, since they do not pay anything for cohabitation, but any woman at all who gives herself to everybody. In view of the promiscuity still rampant among the uncircumcised and unmarried, which is to be considered a survival of that originally universal erotic institution, a woman's giving herself up to several men is nothing unusual so as to necessitate coining a separate word for it, especially considering the poverty of the language; just as little as it would occur to them to designate the man who has relations with several women outside his own, with a separate title. It was only with the introduction of prostitution into the interior of the continent by the Arabs, Indians, Arabized inhabitants of the coast, and finally by the whites that a term entered the vocabulary of the negro that was soon generalized and carried over to his everyday conditions.

Because of the fact that she follows a very lucrative occupation, she is always well dressed, and is the only black person with whom the *msungu,* the white master, condescends to have relations. The prostitute has acquired a high social standing among the negroes, and enjoys a certain measure of respect everywhere, especially among the Bantu tribes. There the word prostitute is even used as a name for girls, and is not considered offensive. I knew a Mnioro woman who called her daughter simply *"Mlaya."*

---

* The following is a typical answer that a coquetish Budama woman gave me when I said to her jokingly that she was a harlot, "I am a whore, you are a whoremaster, we are all whores."

184

Among the Semi-hamites, the Nandi, prostitute is not a title of honor, but neither of shame. Among parents and older people the prostitute is not made conspicuous, because of the sense of shame already referred to. For usually she is a married woman, and does not like publicly to announce to the neighborhood of her parents that she has torn the tie of marriage and run away from her husband.

The Nandi woman seems to be predestined to prostitution. Not so much because of their coquettish nature, but because of the unbearable conditions under which these tortured creatures live. She is mercilessly beaten by her husband, that wales cover her whole body; she must lug indescribably heavy loads that almost break her down. But that is not the worst of it. Very often she is bartered away by her parents to a man who does not appeal to her, indeed, whom she even hates, so that it is an effort on her part to give him her love. Then she is often still half a child; he, on the other hand usually an old drunken fool. Is it any wonder then that she runs away from her old man during the nuptial night and throws herself into the arms of the first white man she meets, but who, the first night, at least, treats her like a human being? I have heard the life story of many prostitutes, and it was always the same: during the night, often the first night, she ran away in her stinking leather dress, from her ugly, decrepit husband, carrying with her her fine ornamentation to some friend living alone. Through the mediation of the latter she came to the Indian, Somali or white man; with the money she bought a new dress, immediately took off her massive iron ornaments and her leather dress, putting on one of cotton. She began a new life far away from her home; she is a *mlaya*.

But she is considered a whore only outside her reservation, among strangers. At home she is still the *osotya*, the circumcised woman, who, if she wishes to give herself to a *moran*, she may not demand or receive any recompense for it.

The Nandi prostitute is differentiated from her sisters in that she speaks Kisuaheli, which no other woman of her tribe speaks—unless she has learned it by chance as the wife of a black servant—and that she wears no leather clothing. If one sees a Nandi woman wearing shoes and dressed in a short sleeved cotton dress, and if she speaks Kisuaheli, one can with assurance say that she is a prostitute. These are the external signs. Besides that she is painstakingly clean, actually washing, ornamenting and anointing herself from morning to night, and standing for hours in front of the mirror.* Her sense of taste is quite well developed too, not only in that she eats foods that are taboo for the other women, such as chicken or eggs, but prepares foods not on the natives' menu, as, for example, unleavened bread baked in oil or butter, rice, tomatoes, tea: foods, the preparation of which she has learned from an Indian or Mohammedan. And she rejects the flesh of fallen animals, while the negroes as a rule do not balk at eating carcasses. She smokes English cigarettes constantly. And lately, especially in Uganda, she began to drink whiskey, which the white man brings to her, because she has no opportunity otherwise of getting it. She does not care for sweets, such as chocolate and bonbons, which is a characteristic of all negroes.

---

* The negress as well as the negro make no use of mirrors. But prostitutes like to have hand mirrors. At a medicineman's, who was a great woman chaser, I discovered a wall mirror.

The prostitute has a fine trait, which is probably latent in every negress as a result of the polygamy of the men and the resulting equality of all women in the harem: she is extremely ready to help her colleagues, she is entirely unselfish, even altruistic. Not only does she always lend her prettiest clothes to her friends, but she often gets a man

90. Brothers

for her, even at her own expense. To speak evil of their friends is something foreign to these dark daughters of Eve, unless their rival belongs to another tribe. And then only moderately.

The negro prostitute lives with a man as his concubine, or with a friend, or, what is more general, in a small room in the prostitutes' quarter, the so-called *pangani*. All these brothels, if they may be so called, look very needy: they have a *style*. Square houses, with scanty clay plastering, so that the boughs of the frame show, with a tin roof of beaten flat oil-cans or of corrugated sheet iron; that is how they look from the outside. Within there are several chambers, a large comfortable bed made of sticks, above it a string, on which all kinds of cloths hang, making a curtain; one or two crude, wooden chairs and some-

times a table. A table lamp, a very large washing basin,
and a simple chest with a hanging lock are always there:
a few strings of glass beads, linen cloths, a mirror, tea,
cigarettes. The tea kettle and one or two porcelain cups
belong in common with several others. That is all the
blacks have. And that is all!

They spend their lives in the *pangani* as if in a ghetto.
Like all prostitutes, they get up late, visit each other, go
to the Indian or to the butcher, the Somali, where they
gossip more than they buy. Then they return home, drink
tea with lots of sugar, eat their round, well-baked, flat
bread with it, play their harps, go to the Indian in the
late afternoon, spending the whole day in *dolce far niente*.
All this while they keep ornamenting and washing themselves. They often have an errand boy who does the most
necessary things for them. They wash their own clothes
at a brook or creek.

Every Saturday evening there is a large festival. In the
public house, near every *pangani*, there is dancing and
drinking of beer. There the dancing is not according to
the negro custom, each sex by itself, but according to the
European fashion in couples. There they appear, slowly
one after the other, particularly well dressed; and the negro dandies come on bicycles from the neighborhood. Even
the black chauffeur is not absent today. On this evening
they often obtain leave, if they are servants, and then
each hurries to his wench. He had paid the monthly ten-
shillings rental for her in advance, and for that he has the
right of claiming the love of his dearest four times a
month. The first time the weekly payment on the part
of the wench for this rental goes off very nicely. Perhaps for the whole first month. Then arguments begin

188

between them. At the Saturday night dance she promised herself to another who paid her more money. She dances with him instead. The lover, vexed, and full of jealousy, insists upon her leaving the *ballroom*, which she does; and now they withdraw. The conversation which they now carry on in her room is very instructive for the better judgment of the prostitute—not to say of the feminine soul. They sit on the bed, she with her head hanging or turned away from him, he constantly repremanding. At first she is silent. Under the pressure of his reproaches her hatred of men grows, the hatred of the oppressed against the oppressor. She is thinking only of him who has been courting her this evening and who would have given her five shillings for one night. That her present friend has already paid her money in advance does not seem to bother her. That was, that belongs to the past, while that of her present lover would increase her capital. In the face of the wench's indifference the somewhat aroused guest begins to rage, and she does not let herself be outdone in retorting.

"Who do you think you are?" she says to him. "I can have hundreds of men, if I wish: Indians, Somali, yes, even *msungus;* what do I want you for?"

That is too much for him. He threatens to set fire to the hut, to give her a thorough beating, if she does not give herself to him. This threat calls forth respect in her; she acts as if she agrees, only she says casually that she must go out to make herself more comfortable, and will soon be back. But she does not come back. She sleeps this night at the house of the first friend she meets.

Prostitution among the blacks needs no protectors. As we have seen, even one apparently her protector must

189

pay for his pleasure of four nights by paying the usual rent. Benefits, as the European pimp enjoys them, who treats his girl heartlessly, like a vampire, are something foreign, unknown among the negroes, which speaks for the independent position and the prestige which a prostitute holds among them.

Nor does the true negro brothel, as we have observed it in Eldoret, Kitale, Nairobi, have that monster, the old matron, to whom the girls must give all their earnings. There is only one master or mistress of a house, one negro family, to whom the monthly rental of ten shillings is paid. Otherwise the black prostitute is a completely independent, self-reliant being. Only the local police control them.

For this purpose, before she rented a room in the *pangani*, she appeared before the chief of the district and told him her decision of becoming a prostitute. The chief of the district asks her several personal questions: whether she felt strong enough to practice the trade, and gave her some instructions, of which we quote the following as being the most important:

"You must not serve two men in one night. If you have one and are sleeping with him, lock your door and let no other in. Tell him through the door you are taken for the night. Otherwise only quarrels and strife would result."

The woman promises the official to follow his instructions, pays ten shillings as a tax for her calling and disappears.

The black *ashkari* (military police) visit the *panganis* regularly, to prevent possible fights. While exercising this duty they are often very free with the girls. In Nairobi the Englishmen asks the *ashkari* on duty to point out a brothel to him or to tell him where there are pretty girls. And the *ashkari* acts very officious. In contrast to the brothels in the capital Nairobi (on the Rout River), those in Eldoret or Kitale are as a rule not visited by whites. They are exclusively negro brothels, only for blacks, seldom for Indians. The men pay two to five shillings for a night. Besides the few Baganda girls, most of the prostitutes are Nandi. In Nairobi, however, the prostitutes are recruited from the Kikuyu. Arab women are also met with. There are no Indian prostitutes in all East Africa.

The houses of joy in Mombassa and Port Said are not representative of conditions in the interior. In the seaports life is fast, and the Arab women, who are most often the prostitutes, cannot be counted among the blacks. They are perverse, or at least may be made to indulge in all kinds of perversities—in Port Said there was a prostitute in the year 1909 who allowed herself to be covered by a he-ass (sic!)—and they look almost like southern Europeans. They are exploited by old women, whom they must give a part of what they earn for clothing, rent and food.

Compared to the black *pangani* a brothel in Mombassa looks almost genteel. There are reception rooms, sofas, soft chairs, and a good broad soft bed. When one enters such a house and he desires to have a cancan danced before him, in which the girls appear naked and execute all kinds of belly movements. They sing at the same time, laugh artificially, beat the tamborine loudly and shake their stomachs and bellies. Five shillings must be paid to every dancer, that is, about twenty to twenty-five for every cancan. If many visitors happen to be present, the cost is divided among them. And *hustling* is a regular procedure: heavy money must be paid for beer and liquor drunk. He who wants to be amused besides must pay extra. The rate is from five to twenty shillings. There are particularly fine sights to be seen in Mombassa at the festival that concludes the month of Ramadan, when the feet, hands, foreheads and cheeks of the prostitutes are decorated with wonderful black or orange-brown ornaments. Out of every brothel in the prostitutes' quarter the harlots beckon to the men in broad daylight. besides the houses of joy there are in the Arab quarter of Port Said private dwellings in which only one prostitute lives. She usually crouches on a stool in front of her house in the evening, balancing herself, like an acrobat, in the oriental fashion, on her legs as they are crossed under her. The black prostitutes in Kampala (Uganda) also live in their own grass huts, usually with a sister or friend.

The inhabitants of the black *panganis* of Kitale and Eldoret are not examined by doctors. If cases of disease, which are not very common, are reported to the chief of police, the sick woman is at once sent to the hospital at Eldoret.

A negro prostitute earns on the average forty to fifty shillings a month. With this money she provides herself with clothes, towels, beads, shoes and stockings; the Indians readily trust her because she is a good customer and they like to flirt with her. The rest of the money is saved for her future subsistence. From time to time she sends her money, which she has deposited with the Indian, to her parents. With it they buy her cattle.

But, according to the complicated civil law of the Nandis, as yet investigated by no jurist, a female can not own cattle or any other property. So when she comes home after some time and asks her father where the money is, or what he had done with it, he answers something like the following:

"I have often bought myself beer for your money and fixed my house, too."

And then he demands more money from his daughter.

91. Young Prostitute

"I have none," she now says to him reproachfully, "I always give you money and still you don't buy a cow for it." But she only says that; she gives him a part of her savings anyway. She gives more to her mother, who then secretly buys her a cow or a goat, but she keeps the secret of its

193

owner from her father. Her brother knows that she possesses cattle, but acts as if he doesn't. Only the little brother and sister furtively show the big sister, who has returned from the city, her cattle.

It is really sad that such a woman cannot fully enjoy the fruits of her labor in her old age. At the death of their father her older brother inherits automatically all the cattle, including that of his sister, and it depends upon his good will whether he gives her anything of her possessions or not.

As a result of the inhuman *laws*, the life of the free girl is very bitter. I know of a tragic case, which, due to that law of inheritance, cost a human life.

A harlot who had saved enough to buy thirty-five cows and forty-nine goats visited her sick mother. She asked her half-brother to slaughter a goat for the sick woman, which he absolutely refused. Thereupon the good daughter herself slaughtered one of her own goats.

"I smell meat," furiously said the brother when he entered the hut and noticed the goat meat.

"I have slaughtered my own goat, since you would not give me any," she answered proudly.

"Since when does a sister own her goats?" he cried in anger, seized a staff and broke it on her. Then he rushed out of his hut for his spear. Trembling with rage and fear, the sister awaited her fate. The brute rushed back like mad, but she anticipated him and cut his throat with a knife. The sick mother died of grief soon afterwards.

The black authorities acted with unbelievable cruelty towards the desperate woman, who acted only in self-defence. They forced her to eat a piece of her brother's flesh.

194

"You have murdered your brother, now you must eat him!"

She obeyed and ate it. She was also punished with imprisonment for several years and is now married to an *ashkari*.

The visit of a prostitute is always on event in the village. She brings tea and sugar with her, gives away cigarettes, and has fine oil for anointing the body. She would like to wear all her clothes at once, so great is her desire to make a fine impression. Strings of strange looking beads cover her neck and arms. She even has shoes and stockings on. She is the favorite of old and young and as a sign of her popularity she is even invited to the beer festival, to which no ordinary young mortal woman may ever gain admission. Even her father, the only one she is afraid of, appreciates her, the salon negress.

It is moving to see with what devotion and love she turns to the younger girls, with what tenderness she treats them, reminding one of the heroine in Sudermann's *Honor* (when the demimonde greets her sister). She gives the half grown children a piece of white cotton cloth that they might take off their dirty leather clothing and dress and feel like human beings. She herself soaps and anoints the youthfully beautiful body of the young girls, as if she wanted to inculcate with every rub: become like myself, become civilized!

She herself would gladly give up her gay life and subject herself to one man, since she has a presentiment of and sees already the loneliness that is to come to her and which haunts her like a ghost. But which of her black friends has enough money to buy her a pack of cigarettes a day and offer her tea? She cannot live without either;

195

nor would she, a free person, let herself be dominated by her husband, much less be beaten. She cannot give up the *benefits of civilization* which she has tasted. She longs for the Saturday night dance in the *pangani*, where she is conscious of her position, and has many dandies at her feet. And she can not live without cigarettes. So her

92. A Prostitute

thoughts run. She returns from the reservation to her second home, to the ghetto of the *pangani*. But her visit to her family brings new recruits for prostitution. Every one of her visits is followed by a flight of girls, one after the other, from the reservation, where the rigor of the law hampers the freedom of woman's every movement, to the *pangani,* where the woman is happy and free.

Even mothers in the reservation are so delighted by the career of her who has come to visit them, that they secretly harbor the wish that their daughters might follow the example of the *mlaya.*

93. Woman Making Pots

MARRIED LIFE

Whoever has spent some time among the shepherd peoples, on a negro reservation, where, undisturbed and uninfluenced by the blessing of missions and other bearers of civilization, the black lives his own life, however much it may be restricted by rites and rules, and whoever has followed their actions with unbiassed eyes, has noticed that a negro's life rotates about women, beer, cattle, and that is all.

The sacred cattle represents his wealth. It supplies him with his daily staple foods: milk, blood and meat. With cows, oxen and goats he buys his wives. And so cattle signifies even more to him, it is the investment of his capital, the means toward an end.

In a woman he sees not only the mother of his children, but above all a source of pleasure, in whom he satisfies his desire, and later a means for work to be exploited. She also makes his beer. In his emotional life he gives his wife so much, or rather so little, only enough to conquer and hold her fast. Otherwise the influence of his wife on the freedom of his actions in everyday life is very slight, if not to say zero. Only the wife's unimportant possessions are respected by her husband. If someone, for example, wishes to buy a calabash, a basket or a piece of ornamentation from him, he says, "See my wife about it." She, on the other hand, does not dare to sell anything without his knowledge. On the possession of children the mother may also decide.

Beer (*tembo* or *pembe*) serves a man not only as food, but lifts him above the prosaic feeling of everyday life into the Dionysiac, makes him potent as a man and it also has the effect of an aphrodisiac (sic!). The drinking festival is his form of worship, in it he finds a substitute for religion: instead of being bound, he is unburdened. And finally in the beer-song, which is not struck up until all have become gay, is expressed the man's will to freedom, his unrestraint, his humanity.

What beer is to the mature or old man, the dance is to the youth. The regular rhythm has an effect similar to that of beer, arouses similar feelings of freedom, unrestraint and masculine power. Each is a game and changes the grown-ups into care-free children. The negro has only one word for dancing and playing, *cheza*.

The circle of the woman's ideas is also filled by those three great questions, cattle, spelt, men. But they press upon her heavy as fate. Cattle is to her a symbol of work: the care of the house, from the painful cleaning of milk calabashes to the sweeping of the cow-stall, the preparation of food, not including the feeding of old and young. One would think that that was enough to fill out a working day. The woman's other sorrow is the cultivation of the soil: clearing of the ground, planting of the spelt, harvesting it, stamping it, and converting it into flour or beer.

Only in her love for her husband, who treats her so inhumanly, she finds a ray of happiness in her otherwise pitiable dark life. Here she feels herself at home, she is no more the beast of burden, the slave, the servant. Here she is in her element and dominates her man, as a being radiating love. She plays the game of love as if she had just come from a Paris salon into the land of the blacks. Humble, sulking, giving herself, refusing—all, as the tactics of the strategy of love demand. The negress desires, as do our women, that she be paid attention to, that she be courted, flattered; she also desires to be conquered. Woman has the same power over man in Africa.

Her age plays no part in her vanity, as with our women, so that she would want to conceal it or reduce it. Moreover, she usually has no idea of how old she is. Negro prostitutes, when asked about their age, like to answer ironically, "A hundred years."

94. A Family Idyll

Infidelity of the Husband and Jealousy

The negress is tender in marriage in spite of her husband's harshness toward her. With what silence, self-sacrifice, and self-denial she obeys every command of her husband! This tactful conduct is dictated more by love than by fear. Even if he demands of her what would break the heart of a European woman, she performs his fervent desire—not out of subservience or fear, be it emphasized, but out of understanding of his nature, which, indeed, is the synonym of true love. The moralist who has not pierced deep enough into the nature of the negro soul, would, of course, in his prejudiced opinion, say of this case: out of indifference and moral depravity. But that is not so. What does her husband demand of her?

Nothing more nor less than that she should get him another woman, perhaps a friend, for his bed. That is the custom among the Nandi: a man has his wife get him a strange woman whom he desires and in whom he presupposes a similar feeling. His wife goes, honestly imparts the desire of her husband, nay more, she even tries to convince the other, if she is undecided. If the other woman explains that she cannot go because she has wood to fetch from the forest, or something of the sort, the legitimate wife helps her to get done with the work sooner.

I know of a case in which the legitimate wife, after executing the command of her husband, hanged herself out of love and jealousy. For every time that her husband had thoughts of infidelity, it cut her to the quick, even though she did not manifest it, nor told her husband about it; she retained her humble devotion. But usually the woman, conquered by her great love for her husband, which gives her a great understanding of him, bears the anguish bravely.

Her connubial home is her best school. She sees that her husband officially marries at least two wives, and more; she herself has already helped her husband, in the courting of a second wife. She knows that the desire for variety, which in the language of the negroes has been given an established expression, "A new vagina is sweet," is dictated by no constant value of love, but rather by the inborn polygamous instinct for new attractions and sensations, in order that feelings, dulled at home by habitual usage, he sharpened and stimulated to new vigor. She knows well that she is the first one her husband married, the first bought, the real mistress, the first lady of the house; the others in the harem are only courtesans. Perhaps her husband assured her that the more women he embraced the more he loved her. But if she is old and through constant penetration into the soul of men has realized that it is absolutely necessary, from the physiological point of view, that her husband satisfy his desire outside the house, she gets him a woman herself, cooks for her, gives her the best milk and the next day even gives her a few *kibuyu* (calabashes) of milk on the way as *bakshish*. But she will not be cheated, she wants to know everything. That is why she raves and rants if her husband happens to cohabit with some woman in the forest without her knowledge. That would be deception, adultery. Whatever happens with her knowledge and consent she does not consider infidelity!

There is a similar relationship among the Baganda. If a woman loves her husband she not only lets him take another into the hut, but actually supplies him with one herself. But if she is jealous she raises a racket and beats the other woman.

The jealous negress is not surpassed in malice by her white sister. I knew a Mohammedan *kamba* whose two upper incisors were missing. When I asked him what happened he said his first wife in a jealous rage broke them out. When she heard that he wanted to marry a second time, she attacked him in his sleep and smashed out his teeth with the massive bracelet on her right arm. He then chased her out of his home for good.

A kind of friendship exists among the women of a negro harem, which usually consists of two members (a negro most often has only one wife). For the most part, a man likes to have his wives separated, and he very often builds them separate huts at some distance apart. I saw some bigamous marriages in which the members lived in huts quite close to each other.

If a man sleeps with one of them, he visits the other one next morning to drink milk out of his fine calabash that is already waiting for him. But he had already drunk milk at the hut of the first. The separation of wives into different huts is probably made more for economical reasons, in order that each might take care of the property entrusted to her, the household, and cattle, rather than out of fear of possible jealousy and strife, for both women usually live together on the best of terms.

Serious quarrels occur only when a woman gives herself to a man without the knowledge of the latter's legal wife. A woman often declines a proposal of love on the ground that she is afraid of his real wife, who would beat her and set fire to her house.

Jealousy may sometimes be the cause of regular quarrels between two women, especially among prostitutes. If she hears that her lover has taken another woman in her absence, she goes to his house to meet her rival. If she finds her, something like the following happens.

"Why are you sleeping with my master?"

"That's not my fault," answers the woman attacked.

"Why did you not refuse him?"

"It is the fault of his rupees, if he loves me. He doesn't get me for nothing. He gave me lots of rupees. Twenty rupees!" This fabulous sum is purposely exaggerated to hurt the rejected woman all the more.

"Really as much as all that?" the latter, tortured with jealously, groans. "My master does not want me any more now!" Then they separate because other woman have gathered around them.

If they meet later, the one deceived usually invites the other to her house. They drink tea.

"Come, accompany me now," says the hostess. Her rival accompanies her.

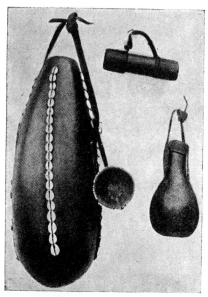

95. Household Implements

"Come, now we'll fight," she suddenly says.

"Why?" the other asks, taken aback.

"Because you are sleeping with my master!"

She then breaks off two rods. "Take your clothes off!" Both undress entirely and let fly at each other. Her rival weakens, the stronger beats her, makes her flee and takes her clothes away. But if her rival is victorious, the poor woman moans, "Now my clothes are gone and she's still sleeping with my master!"

If a man takes his mistress back the cause o f the quarrel disappears of itself. Otherwise the following scene may take place:

"Bring the food," her master says to her.

She is silent.

"I have no food!" he says; "Where is it?" he asks again.

"Go to your sweetheart, she'll give you your food," she finally says.

"Who has told you that I have other sweethearts?"

"Give me a rupee!" she says vehemently, "I don't like gossip."

He then gives her money, and she goes unless he bids her remain. She goes, the other woman comes. Her heart becomes malicious and in the very same night she sets fire to her house.

In such case she does not beat her rival.

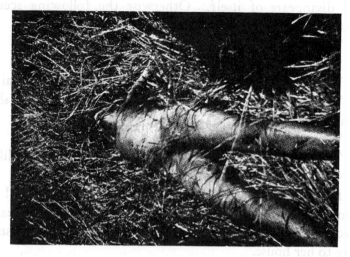

96. Woman Killed for
Infidelity

INFIDELITY OF THE WIFE

We have seen that the husband takes several wives for variety. He tells his latest conquest that he can only be happy with her, that he does not love his former wife. He probably tells the opposite to the latter.

But what about the fidelity of the woman? "Are the wives of negroes true?" This question is often asked; but whether the negro is true to his wife is not asked.

As in Europe, the answer to the problem must depend upon the individual case. If the marriage in question is one of love, the negress is as a rule true to her husband. But when a young girl is married off to an old sot, it can hardly be expected that she be true to him. In such marriages lies the germ of infidelity; out of such marriages come most concubines.

I will relate a horrible, bloody deed of a horned husband as an example to illustrate the natural obnoxiousness of unequal marriages.

A pretty, young woman, who, in true Nandi fashion, had had several affairs with uncircumcised boys before she herself was circumcised, and who was now married to an elderly man, one day, while her husband was drinking beer at a neighbor's, took five such uncircumcised boys(*layoni*) into her hut, with whom she probably slept, one after the other. Each time one of them stood watch at the door, so that they might be ready in case her husband returned home unexpectedly. When it was about ten o'clock at night and the old man still did not appear, the young fellows did not worry about him any more. But in the midst of their pleasure they were surprised by the old man. There was a good brawl out of which the master of the house, of course, emerged victor, for one uncircumcised will hardly dare to life his hand against an old man; the five *layoni* ran away with swelling wales on their bodies, and the woman succeeded in escaping. She spent the rest of the night with a neighbor. The next morning an old man brought the young wife back to her husband. He asked her where she had slept, how she was, and then had her cook porridge. After the meal he took some Cayenne pepper out of a leather wallet and gave it to his wife to grind. His younger brother happened to come in just then and asked him for

"For my brown cow," answered the old man, adding that he was going to slaughter it. His brother left and his wife continued to grind the pepper.

In the evening he said to her, "Bolt the door well and go to sleep, I am going out."

He did not go away but lay in wait in front of the hut. When his wife had fallen asleep he dug himself into his hut with his knife, entered, and lit a fire.

Now his pent up fury got the better of him. He put a noose around the neck of his unsuspecting, sleeping wife, the prey of his unbridled rage and hate, but without pulling it tight, bound her hands and feet, sat her up and began to whet his sword. If he could not have all of her to himself, at least he could mar her beauty. With his sword he made a lateral cut along the right leg, the hip, ribs and the right arm, neck and shoulder, reaching even behind the ear; then a similar one on the left side of the body. The woman, bathed in blood and writhing with pain, groaned fearfully, but he was still not satisfied. In his inhuman thirst for vengeance he rubbed her wounds in with pepper. The neighbors, attracted by the crying and groaning, hurried up and called from the outside, "Don't kill her or the *ashkari* (policeman) will take you away!" That only augmented his fury still more, and he began to make additional parallel cuts on the arms, diagonally, and to rub in with pepper.

Only when the woman collapsed with pain and torture did his rage abate. The inhabitants of the village, dominated by the typical black argument, based on the fetish of legal possession, could not interfere.

"But she's his wife, he bought her!"

The woman became one mass of flesh. She did not die, but could neither lie nor sit. If she sat the flesh of her open wound would stick to the ground or grass, if she lay the wounds had a tendency to grow to the cowhide that served as a bed. She was a direful picture of lost beauty, a warning example to adulteresses and a repulsive attestation of the brutality of a man who was capable neither of loving nor of forgiving.

Another case shows no less cruelty on the part of a deceived husband. A man learned from his brother quite late, not until his wife was in an advanced stage of pregnancy, about her infidelity.

"Your wife," he said to him, "is prostituting herself."

The angry husband gave his wife a horrible beating lasting all day and finally killed her by piercing her neck with his spear. The doctor who was called saved the living child by making an incision in the dead woman. The man was sent to prison for two years for his crime (Nandi).

Adulteresses who are beaten to death are not rare among the Nandi. Usually the poor woman escapes murder by suicide, which occurs quite often among the Nandi, and, as the missionary, Mr. Rees, told me, among the Maragoli. More than the fear of their husbands, the loss of the love of their seducers drives them to suicide.

I knew a woman who committed such a suicide. She had something unusual among negroes: intelligent eyes like those of a Spanish woman. I shall never forget the melancholy glance with which she looked at her surroundings. She was the most beautiful Nandi woman I have ever seen. And how sad it made me when I happened to meet an old friend of hers and learned that she had died the day before.

"But she was thoroughly healthy!" I exclaimed.

"Yes, her husband beat her because she had run away. And so she hanged herself because she hated the old fellow and could not reach her lover."

The police officer at the inquest called my attention to

the remarkable custom of first besprinkling the corpse with cow-dung before freeing it from the string by which it hung. Apparently, in order to pacify the demons.

Not every adultery ends so tragically, or the greater part of the negresses would have been dead long ago.

Among the Bagishu the adulterer must pay the woman's husband two cows or oxen, which does not prevent him from giving his wife a thorough beating anyway. Among the Nandi the greedy husband drives his unfaithful wife out and receives back from his father-in-law all the cows he gave as a dowry. If he is gracious enough to receive her back, her father must atone for her infidelity by paying the husband a cow. The enraged husband may slaughter any number of the adulterer's cattle at night, and no one can do anything about it (Nandi, Sebeyi).

Morans are in the habit of biting through the hanging strands of skin of their rivals' ear lobes, if they are *layoni*. This is not meant to cause pain but to brand the fellow for life as a seducer (Nandi).

I have noticed that among the Bantu the deceived husband does not take his wife's adultery as seriously as the shepherd people. He has bought the woman and therefore, he argues, the adulterer must pay him money as compensation. With him it is quite a business transaction.

Infidelity of women is more widespread among some tribes. At any rate, punishments do not seem to have any influence on the woman's faithfulness, or cases of adultery among the Nandi, where they often end with death, would not be so numerous, while among other tribes (*e.g.*, the Kavirondo) where I have not heard of suicides or murder, adultery is by far less frequent. Even among the Sebeyi, who are quite closely related to the

211

Nandi, adultery is rather unusual. If advances are made to a woman of this tribe, she rejects them, moving her hand quickly across the throat, indicating what her husband would do to her if he found out.

Bagishu women have the rather mean habit of playing with fire before they reject their admirers. At first they skilfully submit, promise to give themselves to them for a stipulated price, but, of course, like every negress, want to be paid in advance. When she has the money in her possession she runs with it triumphantly to her husband and gives it to him ,who is overjoyed at the cleverness of his wife, but still more at the *price of sin* obtained by swindling. They do that to whites as well as blacks. It never occurs to the husband that his wife, the skilled intrigante, may cheat him the very next day by giving herself for nothing to the man whom she loves, or to someone who won't let himself be cheated.

When one thinks of the love-life of negroes he must always remember that the negro, and even more so the negress, acts very undiplomatically, imprudently, and is even loquacious in these matters, which among us require great care, secrecy and silence. A love affair may actually take place right before the eyes of everyone. If a woman is unfaithful, the whole village usually knows it. Not that the negro would be so unchivalrous as to prate about his successes, he says no word about them. The others take care of that. Old women who over-heard the conversation he had with the woman, the children who were standing by when he asked her. Only those who are of the same age are silent and generally take the side of the seducer and the seduced.

The following love affair took place before my very

eyes. Of course it was at a beer festival. Among the
guests there was especially conspicuous a medicineman in
the very flower of manhood. He was twenty-seven years
old, bigamous, and a passionate woman chaser. He had
left his two pretty wives at home. What would he want
with them at his friend's beer party? There was always
some pretty woman or other there, and no Nandi female
could resist his handsomeness.

A medicineman wields an almost magical power over
the blacks of his tribe. Even when he is old and ugly.
They are afraid that he might enchant them with sterility,
disease, and even punish them with death. They therefore try to win his good will by love. The medicinemen
are a veritable plague for they terrorize the whole neighborhood, and, thanks to their prestige, they know well
how to exploit it for their own benefit. For this very
reason, they are hated by the men, especially the old ones.
If a medicineman wants a woman it is almost impossible
for the girl's father to deny her to him, for a wife or only
for a few nights. He, the medicineman, first calls together
his staff of body-guards and speaks to them in metaphors,
something like this: "In this and this village is a little bird.
I want it!" That is all he says. But that is sufficient to
let his *ashkaris*, or however one wishes to call his handy
men, to guess his desire. They set out at once to find the
woman or girl in question, impart to her the will of their
master, and finally arrange a meeting between the medicineman and the girl's father, over beer, of course. Whenever the medicineman demands beer,* it must stand ready
for him, or the cattle would perish in an epidemic, rain

* This is often an expensive affair, since beer is understood to mean a drinking
party from eleven o'clock in the forenoon to midnight for at least ten people.

would not fall on the spelt fields, lions would break into the corrals.

This time our medicineman had ordered beer at a friend's home, and appeared with his retinue. The girl whom he desired to have for that night was present. But today she was unfortunately in tight hands; fate may successfully maintain itself even against the magical power of a medicineman.

But a beer fete without a woman at the end was for *Ar-ap Kenda,* the medicineman, as incomprehensible as dancing without singing, a thunder storm without lightning. Among the guests, however, another couple was present who came from another related tribe, the Aldai, and had come from some distance. The man seemed to be a good natured, upright old fellow. His wife was in her late twenties, her eyes had that peculiar glitter, betraying the usual fire that flares up from the depths of a woman of this age, a fire that still has the power of enkindling those about her.

While her husband sat at his beer within, she conversed outside with the girl who was to be had that night.

"Do you know," the Aldai said to the Nandi woman, "he pleases me very much."

"And he likes you immensely," lied the girl, in order thereby to provide a woman for her darling.

"Really?" answered the elder woman, as if embarrassed, "I'd very much like to have him, but I have a daughter at home, too, and so, you know . . ." She was referring to the fact that in such a case she could never give him her daughter to wife, for among the shepherd peoples the mother-in-law is taboo for the son-in-law.

"But how can you leave him in the lurch now," lied

214

the Nandi woman, "he has assured me that he wants you immensely."

The little intrigante then stepped into the hut and whispered into *Ar-ap Kenda's* ear that the older woman would like to sleep with him that night. The old Aldai had not the slightest idea of what was going on about him but kept sucking gaily on his straw. Then the woman with the peculiar fire in her eyes entered the hut. A general whispering, and low giggle, went from one person to the other. But it stopped at the good, old Aldai; he heard nothing, understood nothing. His wife, however, laughed secretly also; it was a laugh of confusion, for she did not know whether her husband noticed anything, or she was being fooled, or she was really to have *Ar-ap Kenda.* She gladly accepted the last.

There was flirting and whispering the whole evening: the black Don Juan sat motionless on his cowhide and drank with the old man; she, nervous on account of the love-adventure before her, kept leaving the hut to confer with her friend outside. When it got late she took leave. Without saying a word she went out. *Ar-ap Kenda,* who still acted as if unaffected by the coming event, had decided that she was to sleep in the other half of the hut, separated by a wall, and in which usually calves and goats spent the night. But the small door from the room to the other half was open and right before it the old man sucked his straw. *Ar-ap Kenda* noticed it and became a bit nervous. But this hindrance was done away with also. The girl who had set the whole affair going whispered something to the mistress of the house and the small door, consisting of one board, was shoved between the wicker-work of the wall. Now the drinking began in real earnest.

It was not until after midnight that the old man drank enough; he said good-bye and went his way. *Ar-ap Kenda* took his night meal and disappeared to the elderly woman.

The next day I learned that it was only very much against her will that the Aldai woman had consented to spend a night of love in the goat house with *Ar-ap Kenda*. When she left the hut she decided to go to the family whither she had been invited with her husband; so she went through the dark night into the village. But the mistress of the house had hurried after her and had convinced her to return, indicating that her husband had said that he would spend the night in her house.

The next morning the whole village knew about it; the husband also. But he did not beat her for she had always, up to this time, been faithful to him and he knew that the fault lay entirely with the medicineman, who acted as if he had sacrificed himself for the sake of the woman.

This faithfully, perhaps too diffusedly, told story shows how openly the preparations for adultery are made: everyone helps the bold adulterer, no one warns the husband.

Among the Suaheli, as was told me by many people, but which I have not been able to verify, there is even an instrument in general use for accomplishing shameless adultery. In the yard, near the fence, there is a gate-like board in which there is a hole about a yard from the ground. Early in the morning the negress takes her stand there with her back to the board and facing her husband, who, though still lying in the hut, can watch her well from his bed. Her lover comes to the gate as prearranged, she bends down forward, acts as if she were washing the cooking utensils, and calls out some chance phrase to her husband, who suspects nothing, while her lover has her through the hole in the board. "He has a hole in her board," which sounds like Boccaccio.

The Bantu women with their Hottentott aprons are much looser than the circumcised women of the shepherd peoples. No man is sure of his wife there. He has therefore introduced the practice of having the young or newly-wedded woman accompanied by a small boy who watches her like an argus and reports to her husband all her conversations (Baganda, Budama).

If a widow lives with her son, he believes it his duty, though he partakes of every erotic freedom himself, to exercise control over her as a moral censor. I thus knew an old woman, the mother of a medicineman, who was as ugly as an hyena, but who still knew how to attract men and found pleasure in the act. Among the many affairs she had with various men, the sultan of the village occupied a privileged position. He visited her repeatedly at night, and, as is the custom among the Nandi, left his spear outside sticking in the ground. One evening the medicineman noticed the spear in front of his mother's hut, hid it, without saying a word, and when the sultan of the village left, gave his mother a good beating.

Now the sultan went hunting for his spear, but was unsuccessful. Since it is something unheard of for a spear thus stuck in front of a hut to be stolen, the sultan finally called the *elders* of the village together to take some stand on this theft. The medicineman appeared at the session with the spear and handed it over to him without saying a word.

The sultan had to pay the medicineman an ox as a fine and give him beer. The latter's mother was not invited to this feast, but the sultan of the village, on the other hand, was the guest of honor.

From these examples, which I could easily increase by a dozen, we form a clear picture of the fidelity of negroes, and the varied behaviour of both sexes in the case of adultery. The husband, who seems to have free license to all transgressions, punishes his unfaithful wife very severely, sometimes driving her even to suicide, and collects high fines from his rival for the deed. But that a black should commit suicide out of love or jealousy for his wife, has not been heard of to this day.

The husband is brutal, egoistic and despotic in his love. To him his wife is in every respect, but especially socially, a being of lower plane. That is shown even in eating: he drinks his fill of milk, but often denies it to his wife, who must eat her porridge dry. The relationship of the sexes for every vital question is correctly symbolized by the large, beautiful calabash of the husband, ornamented with cowrie-shells and strings of beads, as contrasted with the ugly, little one of his wife, that has no ornamentation at all.

97. Masturbating Boy

FEMININE LOVE, MASCULINE POTENCY AND ONANISM

The black woman loves her husband, clings to him like a child to its mother, fears him like a servant his master. Only when married life becomes unbearable, especially as a result of marriages arranged against the girl's will by her parents, as is too often the case, does the woman become an independent being, frees herself from the yoke that crushes her physically and psychically and becomes a concubine and prostitute.

Even girls who do not know whether their beloved will marry them, often manifest strong love, in obedience to their hearts. They actually run after the youth or *moran* whom they have given their love.

When the world war seized its bloody victims below the equator, and the Nandi were conscripted like cattle going to slaughter, it was not at all unusual to see girls who had followed their lovers from Kapsabet to Kismu on the Victoria Nyanza, about fifty miles, "in order to die with their lovers." It was not until the *ashkaris* interfered that the girls and women were forced to return.

Like every woman, the black is capable of true love. With unbridled passion in a state of aroused emotion, she quite resembles the white woman. No barrier is too great for her when she desires to attain her end. For the black is very exclusive in his race-consciousness. This exclusiveness may go so far that a woman who has intercourse with a man of another race may be most maliciously persecuted by her own people. Even among members of one and the same tribe, those who have different totems may not marry those of another (Nandi). If a woman loves a man of another race, she already finds herself in a tragic conflict. I know a case of this kind. A Wandorobbo woman had married a Kikuyu *moran;* in revenge the members of her tribe tore her eyes out. Nevertheless this horrible example did not deter a neighboring woman. She left her husband, with whom she had had two children, in order entirely to give herself to a handsome Kikuyu. After lengthy negotiations between the man by whom the Kikuyu was employed, the deceived husband, the enterprising woman and the bold seducer, the woman was finally brought back to her home. I could not tell from the woman, as she stood in front of her low hut of leaves in the primeval forest, surrounded by her little children and phlegmatic husband, that there had been an intense, but unsuccessful love affair in her life, so happy did she look. One would think she had forgotten her lover, when she had her home before her. But the woman later confessed to Mrs. Lindstrom, on whose estate I had the opportunity of studying the family, that she could never forget her lover, so much did she love him.

Naturally, masculine potency has a good deal to do with the strength of the love relationship. Among the Baganda, if a man does not cohabit with his wife she does not cook for him, but if he satisfies her she cooks his meat even at dawn, or kills a chicken for him, even if she has to borrow one from a neighbor. The Bagishu wife is actually vexed if her husband does not sleep with her at night and at dawn. She shouts and complains about it quite loudly, so that the neighbors hear it.

"Maybe my husband's little one is dead, maybe it's an (H)Anisi!"*

By *Hanisi* the black means one who is entirely impotent, one of either sex who is as a rule absolutely passive.

For the Bagishu woman with her Hottentott apron makes great demands of her husband's capabilities; she is hardly ever satisfied. I was told about a case in Mbale (Uganda), in which a Bagishu woman slept with ten men one after the other and perished in the embrace of the last one. The white authorities could not punish the men because it turned out that she was a nymphomanic and had run after the men. Rape is usually punished by seven years imprisonment. But considering how easy the women are, it very seldom occurs.

All kinds of exaggerated stories are in circulation about the potency of the men. I was assured by Nandi *morans* that they had their wives twenty times in one night, especially when they had eaten a good deal of meat and

---

* Borrowed from the Arabic.

drunk much beer. This is certainly a bluff. On the contrary, through questioning of conscientious negroes and of women who did not boast I came to the conviction that the black is very moderate in sexual intercourse: three times in one night is a real accomplishment for him. That was also confirmed by a candid husband, the father of six children (Mgishu). "If my wife wants a child, we do it three times during the night," he added. Negro prostitutes also told me that a negro cohabits only once or twice a night. Of course, it may occur that once in a while some sensuous fellow sets a record, but that is certainly an exception.

A newly wedded Elkoyni, who had a very pretty, sensuous young wife, once came to me with a great request: he asked that I give him a medicine so that he could have his wife twelve times in succession. I smiled at his strange wish and as a joke gave him some *hypermanganate of potash* for external treatment, whereupon he was overjoyed. Several days later I met him. He smiled, the liar, as if it had helped him.

Impotence may lead to suicide. A young Mgishu became impotent, and as a result could not satisfy his wife. "I come to you that you may take me!" she said to him. "I am not your sister!" "What's wrong again, that you don't fill me!" she shouted.

He was silent, then he said he was going to bathe; instead of that he hanged himself.

The more I observed negroes, the more I became convinced that they are not erotically promiscuous libertines, but rather that they are normal and moderate in their sexual desires. Otherwise they would have acquainted the women with all kinds of perversities, which are practically unknown. The very fact that the negro never touches his wife's sexual parts, and that he does not know how to make full use of her erogenetic zones, speaks distinctly enough for the correctness of my assertion. The only thing deviating from normal coitus in which he finds pleasure is having his wife ride him, as she executes the Suaheli milling movement facing him (especially widespread among the population of Uganda). It is also said, especially by highly uncritical farmers, that it is quite customary among the negroes not to withdraw at the end of the act, but to leave it in the whole night; but upon many questionings I was assured by both men and women that this report, like so many others, was absolutely unfounded. Only in the case of stolen love, does he do it in a standing posture when someone is nearby for he is afraid of being surprised.

Masturbation is not as wide-spread among negroes as in other places. It is confined almost exclusively to young people; among the Bantu tribes more than among the Semi-hamites. The very fact that the negro is ashamed of this physiological process, keeps it a secret, and considers it something bad, while he speaks openly about all other expressions of the sexual life, proves what disgust he has for it.

It is really only children who practice masturbation. Among the Semi-hamites it occurs more from the desire of having the foreskin drawn back, in order to resemble the older folks, than to satisfy awakening desires. Among the Nandi it is common practice for the boys to smear the sticky, milky juice of the euphorbiaceous plant *yeptiringuet*, on the glans and to masturbate (*lat pertit*). The juice of this plant is quite caustic and causes the glans to

223

swell strongly, so that the foreskin can easily be drawn back, which is what is wanted. During this process the boys call out "Become large, and I'll give you something to eat." ("*Suren, suren, ce kwamon pek a metet.*") Then the little boy can go to a girl and try it.

Among the Sebeyi, onanism (*kirre*) is very widespread among the youth. But as they get older they stop, especially since they believe that the children of masturbators die very early.

Bagishu boys often masturbate in groups in the woods while tending the goats. If they are caught by their parents they are punished.

"How can you take your penis into the same hand with which you eat?" they hear in reproach. That is why their mother will not eat together with them. "You have done something bad,," she says. Little girls run away from masturbating boys, out of fear of being raped.

The boys begin to masturbate, approximately, in their ninth year. They always do it in a crouching position. If he can get an erection he rolls his little rod between the palms of his hands until it stands up. Then he draws the skin down and spits on the glans with perfect precision, using saliva as a substitute for vaseline to lessen the friction. They are so young that they have no ejaculations in this *game* as they call it.

Seldom, if ever, does a *moran* masturbate.

The girls of the shepherd peoples also masturbate until they are circumcised. It is also considered unclean by them to touch the vagina with the hand. If they are surprised by the boys while at this pastime, they are copulated without further ado. The Nandi girls masturbate with the yellow-blossomed *sedum* (*kuserguet*), a succulent plant, from which they have removed the bast. Among the Bagishu it occurred that two young sisters masturbated each other with the skinned, unripe fruits of the banana. One of their brothers who came upon them heard the one who had not yet been satisfied say to the one who had, "Now copulate me!" He drove them apart, but their parents did not punsh them.

Among the Maragoli, *onanism* of the girls is called *"kuikunda kitere"* (*i.e.*, cohabitation with the finger), in contradistinction to that of the boys *"kueniola."* In this designation of the verb, the technique of masturbation is indicated.

Among the Bantu tribes onanism is much more widespread among girls than among the Semi-hamites. Onanistic manipulations are indispensible in the very formation of the Hottentott apron. Is it any wonder then that married women often find pleasure in it when their husbands go cold during coitus, while they are just becoming aroused; that they pluck the India-rubber bands of their hypertelica so long that the longed for detumescence finally does set in?

Among the Semi-hamitic circumcised women and the kindered tribes, masturbation is seldom, if ever, practiced. They cannot stand to have their sexual parts touched with the hand, much less would they undertake any kinetic manipulations of them. Their sense of modesty, their feminine dignity would be deeply injured.

98. Woman with Lip
Ornaments

TRIBADY AND PEDERASTY

"Once," thus a Nandi woman told me of her own ac-
cord, "all the men went to war, and left all the women
behind. A very great number of women remained at
home. They called loudly, "Come! Cohabit with me!"
"With what are we to cohabit with you?" was the answer. A woman came, slept with another, but slept with
her in vain, for both had but the woman's organ. Others
desired more, but were not satisfied. They went and

broke off fresh boughs, cut them to the size and shape of the male's member, and now they began to satisfy each other with it, alternately."

This story, reproduced word for word, is the only case I know of a tribadiac orgy. The mutual masturbation of the two Bagishu sisters has nothing of tribady in it. Both cases, however, are not aberrations, but refined forms of masturbation. Among the men cases of homosexual acts occur, which can not be explained, like the above cases of tribady, by hunger for the heterosexual which can not be satisfied, but are the expression of true homosexual love. These psychic aberrations are encouraged by the feminine appearance of many negroes, as well as by the occurrence of gynandromorphic individuals (*hanisi*). The rather uniform clothes worn often cause girls to appear boyish, and, on the other hand, boys to appear maidenly. Feminine breasts with nipples standing out from pads of fat are nothing unusual among youths (Nandi, Badama, Baganda). In addition to their womanly conduct, their desire for ornamentation, coquettish gestures, and finally the frequent sleeping together of youths in one bed, all favor the psychological bent of one inclined towards homosexuality, and may set one sexually indifferent into the ways of pederasty.

Gynandrians were described to me among the negroes as impotent fellows with feminine manners. These are men, as the negro vividly expresses himself, "whose penis has died," *i.e.*, they are not capable of having erections. There are such individuals in many villages. "His is always hanging because he is a woman." the narrator added drastically. They often go dressed as women, always sleep with the women and girls; indeed, they even cook and attend to other feminine matters. From the various descriptions of these masculine impotents one gets the impression that they are passive pederasts. When I suggested that they migh be hermaphrodites, the negroes I was questioning answered that they knew quite well how to distinguish between hermaphrodites and these intermediate forms. "I know," said one of them to me, "I myself saw such a one in Uganda, he was like a hyena,* half man, half woman, had both sexual parts and the breasts of a woman."

Among the Bagishu they are quite numerous and are called "*mzili*"; among the Maragoli *kiziri*. A seventeen year old boy told me, without being at all embarrassed, that he had cohabited with such a *mzili* in the rear. The passive fellow had called him and given him ten shillings for this short pastime. While he was cohabiting with him, the latter had his flabby member tied up on his stomach. "There are many such masculine prostitutes who have bothered me with similar requests," he continued. "Whereupon I answered them, such as we don't want your behind." The narrator did not give the impression of being a liar, and when I brought his deed to his attention, and asked him how he could ever have done such a thing, he answered me with a typical negro argument, "But he paid me ten† shillings for it," didn't he?"

An absolutely normal Mgisho boy thus described a passive pederast to me, "His buttocks are as dry as wood." The missionary, Mr. Rees, told me of several cases of

---

* The negroes consider the hyena a hermaphrodite because the clitoris of the she-hyena hangs down quite a bit, which is erroneously identified by the blacks with the penis.

† The report of such a large sum seems to me to be exaggerated. If it is true, it is a further proof of how disgusting the execution of such an aberrant act is to the black. Otherwise he would have done it for a lower price.

homoerotic elderly bachelors among the Maragoli. In South Africa, where he had formerly been active, he said pederasty was much more wide-spread.

Among the Nandi several cases of homosexual love are known to me. One of them ended in a killing. A now old man in his youth, lay in the men's house with his girl. Suddenly he noticed that someone was approaching him from behind with unambiguous intentions. Enraged at this, he struck him dead and kept on striking the dead body until he was dragged away.

Another case told me was quite similar. Here also it was the case of disturbing a loving couple in an obtrusive manner. He was not killed, but bound and given a good beating.

On the place of a well known farmer Fj............d, so his friend told me, there was employed a homosexual boy of the Kikuyu tribe, who loved another boy so much that he gladly gave him all his wages. He loved him like a woman so that he got himself too sore to sit down.

Active pederasts are called *onek*.

In Uganda I saw two boys, a Mgisho and a Baganda, lying in bed together in a tent for the siesta, whereupon another boy called it to my attention with the words, "They love each other like husband and wife." When one of the boys was embarrassed before me and objected, the boys deriding them answered quite rightly, "A man does not sleep with another boy in broad daylight."

That the debauchee who is not black finds here a rich field for the satisfaction of his lusts is obvious, especially since he, the master, may do what he wants with impunity. Nowadays the negro is afraid of him and would not dare, as he did thirty or forty years ago, to strike him dead for it. *Ar-ap Kyemotya*, an old man much respected among the Nandi, told me that many years ago, a white man, apparently an Englishman, had broken into his corral, approached a *moran* very importunately, and kept trying to drive him away from his wife, until the latter killed him with his spear. "He insisted upon cohabiting with him in the back," he added laughingly. We see that the Nandi make short work of such a matter.

In Mbale (Uganda), a Baganda woman told me, and this has been confirmed by whites, that just at the time of my arrival, an Indian had seduced his boy to pederasty. He paid him forty shillings for it, but hurt him so, that he bled and died of the contracted wounds. But the boy accused him to an *ashkari* and he was sent to jail for seven years.

Just as the negroes know the black sheep among themselves, they often gave me the names of all whites who had homosexual intercourse with black boys. One of these farmers, in Soy, was having an affair with a Nandi boy that had lasted several years. Even when the latter finally married, his master continued his practices, so that the black fellow today shares his nuptial bed between his wife and his master.

In this, as in other cases, the blacks are not necessarily homosexually inclined; they do it simply for love of gain.

But most are honest and decent fellows, who, even under the threat of dismissal, will not allow themselves to be seduced by their masters. The abnormal in sexual life is despised in Africa.

99. Black-White Bastard

SODOMY

The sense of decency among the blacks, fundamentally normal in their sexual life, is repelled especially by sodomitic acts, which are punished severely.

That is why such cases are not heard of even when they do occur. One always covers up such matters pretty quick. How much truth there is in the stories told about the Somali "covering" she-asses, the Kavirondo cows, the Nandi goats, I do not venture to decide. My Uganda boy, who was an *ashkari* for a time, maintained quite definitely that he had once surprised a Bantu of the Kavirondo tribe with a cow.

231

That the blacks, as true of all nature's children, know thoroughly the *genitalia* of animals,* is proved by what they say about the vagina of the zebra, the clitoris of the hyena, or the penis of the ape, "which looks just like that of a human being." It may be possible that such study arouses sodomitic desires in a weakling with pathologic tendencies, which he can not resist. He finds a good argument for the justification of his acts in the negro's "pantheistic" conception of nature, which draws no sharp division lines between man and animal, and sees no important difference between them. Not to say anything of the alleged power of the rule of "over the cross," strongly propagandized recently from a certain quarter. Is it any wonder then, that a shepherd boy with heated imagination, tired of masturbating, finally attacks a goat or a calf?

Such arguments are popular in the wide-spread sodomitic area of the Suaheli. I have been told by many people, white and black, that the Suaheli and Arabians of the coast, especially around Mombassa, are notorious for their sodomitic acts on slain sea-cows (dugong). The missionaries had a hard job in combating this kind of necrophilous sodomy.

This bestial lechery is motivated, according to the reports, by a superstition, in whose power the poor psychopaths are supposed to be. It was absolutely necessary for the hunter of the dugong to cohabit with the dead animal, or at the next catch he would be dragged into the depths of the sea by a sister animal. But cohabitation with the

---

* Especially of domestic animals. This observation, particularly of ruttish stallions, bulls, etc., probably gave the first impetus to the circumcision of the prepuce.

dead prey would insure him for the future against any such accident on the open sea. This sodomy, consequently, is an act of magic, a preventive act, safeguarding act.

Superstition or otherwise, according to many reports the dugong, when landed, is mounted by none but fishermen. This is such a general occurrence that the people who buy the meat of the sea-cow make the Islamitic fisherman swear by the Koran that he has had no intercourse with the sea-cow he is offering for sale. They do not buy the meat from him unless he swears. They do not want the flesh of a creature that has served man as a beast of pleasure. That is cannibalism.

Even though this story was told me by many people, almost the same in all versions, a negro told me that a white man had even photographed such a sodomite *in flagranti*—it still seems so unbelievable to me, that I can only relate it to the universally known stories of mermaids. It is noteworthy that none of my black guarantors could find anything disgusting in the revolting act of those fishermen. An old, religious, "sexually quite normal" Islamite of the Kamba tribe even told me he would do it too, because the sea-cow had breasts* and a vagina like those of a woman. A fine conclusion drawn by analogy, from the alleged presence of two similar and equally erogenetic organs in man and animals, and thus postulating and allowing a like function between them.

---

* The females of the elephant, the bat and the ape also have their breasts on the thoray, like the human being.

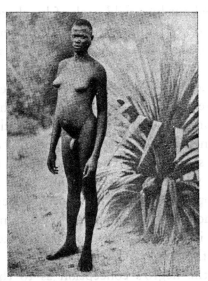

100. Hermaphrodite

VENEREAL DISEASES

In every evil, every pain there is a demon, an evil spirit. It haunts every place; it torments the poor negro, so that he is nowhere safe from it.

Even death, the most natural thing of all natural things, they often blame the demon with. A sorcerer, even a witch, has power over this evil demon. It depends on him, on her, whether the child, the woman, the cow will die or become sick. Therefore the people suspected of witchcraft are shunned.

"Go out of their way!" How often was that not whispered to me in a warning voice! And if a woman dies suddenly, the culprit is immediately found who has enchanted her, who has given her a pernicious medicine (*dava*), which does not always have to be visible. The witch is dragged out by a wild pack of lynchers, two staffs are made fast to her temples, then she is beaten, whipped, burned, so that she usually succumbs to this mob justice (Nandi).

Curiously enough, demons are not considered to be the provokers of venereal diseases. While the slightest feeling of illness is immediately attributed to a witch, her *dava* or evil eye, venereal diseases are brought into direct relation with the sexual act. The blacks know that. It is known in the village, who has syphilis, who has gonorrhea; these people are avoided like lepers. They must live isolated, and no one will knowingly give him or herself to them. But in other respects no care is taken in social contacts with those infected.

Typical to the negro's conception as to the cause of venereal diseases is the conduct of a Uganda boy who had syphilis but who did nothing about it. His master, a friend of mine, repeatedly attempted to have him go to a doctor to be treated, but the boy refused on the ground that:

"God wills it so."

In this Job-like answer there is more religion than is the conception of the average European as to the cause of venereal disease. Among us, syphilis is the work of the evil one, the devil—with him it is the sign of God. The boy was sent to the village hospital. But the Indian physician had to dismiss him because he refused every medical treatment.

Even among the women infected there is a strict moral code, for which one would seek in vain in a European coquette. If one asks a black prostitute whether she is sick, she answers evasively, in case she is, "I don't know whether I'm sick," which means, "I am sick," or she bares her sexual parts, which are perhaps covered with all kinds of ugly eruptions. This honesty is frequently the cause of hunger.

But if she is healthy, she takes a bunch of grass, that is if she is a Nandi, and tries to break it, which is equivalent to taking an oath; if she is a Bantu she likewise answers in negro fashion, evading with a counter-question, "Since when does a sick woman sleep with a man?"

Of syphilis (*tego*) among the negro the whites are *fully enlightened* that it is ninety per cent everywhere: in Uganda as well as in Abyssinia. But how this statistical information has been arrived at is absolutely unknown to me. One repeats it after the other, with the thought in back of his head of scaring the white man, to keep him from having intercourse with the blacks, or to warn him. It is very strange that those who do the warning traffic with the ten per cent who are not infected.

During my two years' stay I met very few sick people: and they were always pointed at. To be sure, in Africa, syphilis is not so bad as it is among us, it usually stops in its primary stage. The negroes maintain that they can effectively cure it with their primitive medicines—all kinds of decoctions—and the farmers confirm the correctness of their statements. At the missions the sick are given iodine (*potassium iodide*) and at the negro hospitals, where the syphilitics are sent by the English authorities, salvarsan is used with great success.

It is remarkable that the Arabian* disease is not more wide-spread than it actually is, considering the careless-

---

* Just as the Germans speak of the French disease, the negroes call syphilis the Arabian disease. Both nations are considered in both cases to be spreaders or introducers of that evil.

ness of those infected. How easy it is for contagion to come about at the beer party, where the straw goes from mouth to mouth! Or from spitting on the hand before shaking, which is considered a particularly hearty form of welcome among the Semi-hamitic shepherd peoples (Nandi).

Gonorrhea (*kisonono* of the Suaheli, *nsugu* of the Baganda) is considered by the negroes—apparently on account of the greater and more lasting pain—to be a much more dangerous disease than syphilis. Every tribe has its medicine for it. Thus the Bagishu use a decoction from the root of the castor-oil plant; others take the poisonous fruits of a *solanum*; the Nandi, on the other hand are supposed to have found a good remedy from the bark of a tree I do not know. By means of a short straw the decoction is first taken into the mouth, not swallowed, but squirted from the mouth directly on or into the genital.

In small children there often occurs a morbid swelling of the glans, which probably arises from putting poisonous saps on the penis. In one case it was caused by the introduction of the glans into the small hole of a two-penny piece; the highly swollen glans could not be withdrawn again. The missionary who was called fortunately was able to cut the coin with a pair of pliers and thus saved the child from danger (Maragoli).

Finally I mention a remarkable therapeutic treatment for snake-bites because it falls within the scope of my sexual researches.

Among the Nandi, who allegedly have an excellent remedy against snake-bites, one who has been bitten by a poisonous snake and does not happen to have the remedy at hand, is to cohabit with a woman. The increased ac-

tivity of the heart as the result of coitus is said to counter-
act the deadly affects of the snake poison. We take alcohol, the blacks take women.

Only a physician with the morbid imagination of the
author of the *Mask of the Red Death* could hit upon the
idea of a similar prophylactic against deadly poisoning,
to which naive observation of the children of nature, held
fast in the sexual-magic view of life, easily came.

101. Negro Brothel

White-Black Bastardy

The question of the sexual relations of the whites with the blacks is the most vital one in all colonial politics because it influences the physical as well as the mental welfare of the white colonists (that of the blacks does not matter anyway) but it was never discussed openly before for hypocritical reasons.

It will exist, in spite of all attempts to cover it up, as long as the sexual instinct, seeking satisfaction, exists in the white man and woman.

Imagine legion after legion of young, enterprising adventurers suddenly let loose in the Eldorado, the free land they have dreamt of. He, who for the most part left *home* to be free of the moral pressure binding him to rigid precepts, to ignore it all, now all at once becomes the *lord* in Africa, a great institution for improvement, according to his parents.

All at once fantastic *latifundia* spread out before him,

a nobody without backbone, a good for nothing and fit for nothing. Now hundreds of black slaves cower at his feet. They, the black peasants, work for him, the white trash.

The more thanks he owes the negro for his prosperity, the more he exploits him, the greater becomes his disdain. He ridicules every good in these black benefactors, without whom he could not take a step safely, could not cultivate one inch of ground—how these black workers are hated by him! The surplus of his hatred he pours out on the missions and the officers of the government, because they open the eyes of the negro, treat him humanely, protect him against complete oppression, cruelty, and also watch the dirty fingers of the white farmer. To the white planter the negro is no more nor less than a wild beast, upon whom he forces culture in order the better to exploit his working power for his own interests. Otherwise the negro does not exist for him at all.

Now let us return to our original point, the real question.

This white trash, fond of life, who at the end of a day's work find distraction in sport, hunting, cards and especially in a rich supply of liquor, at first live for months, indeed, even a year, without any sexual intercourse, since no desired opportunity presents itself to them: they are usually bachelors and it is almost impossible for them to get white women. The easy life under the tropic sun, which in itself loosens the bridles of sensuousness, the copious indulgence in liquor, the involuntary, long-lasting sexual abstinence, being daily surrounded by voluptuous, naked and half-naked women, all this drives towards an eruption and volcanic discharge of the sexual passions.

And now one day for this white man, with his master-morality, arises an apparent dramatic conflict: I say apparent because he does not conceive it to be such. He, the white master, the lord, the *bwana mkubwa* "the big master" must depend upon the black woman. At first it requires great self-control to ignore a prejudice that is deeply ingrained in his race, and share his bed with a black woman. An utterance that a fop once let fall in my presence is very significant in this respect.

"I must always get good and drunk before I take a black woman."

It is a question now which of the two is more human, the black slave, who, having no idea of anything bad, gives herself entirely to her white "sweetheart," or the white man, who must have recourse to whiskey to overcome his disgust, be it even justified, because he has been thus brought up, before he can undertake an act of love.

Nor can it at all surprise one, if in the face o f such an utterance, another farmer thus expresses his opinion:

"Sleeping with a negress is the same as sleeping with a she-ape."

Or that a third who coined this priceless sentence:

"Whoever has intercourse with a negress is perverse."

But those are only prejudices of imagination unsupported by experience.

Once the ice is broken, once the white man has condescended to a passing mesalliance, then he begins to imbibe the poisonous enchantment which black Eve knows only to well how to prepare. He revises his false, prejudiced opinion, and though a few days ago he thought it impossible to touch a black woman, I hear him exaggerating today:

"No white woman does it so well!"

There is no denying it, that in the course of time, after the trial of his race mentality and the succeeding reevaluation of his emotions, a strong attraction and passion for the black woman takes possession of him, taking the place of his former disdain and hatred. Thus there gradually arise from these loose nights of love closer relationships, which often last years, even decades, and finally—of course, seldom,—*degenerate* into true ties of love. Thus it happens that every old bachelor who has been in Africa for years rests in faithful black hands.

But many a married man also makes an excursion once in a while to a black woman. Not only when his wife is spending her vacation in Europe, the distant, legendary *Uleya,* but also when she is at home. It even happens that a white man employs a black girl as a *boy,* who in boy's clothing, short pants, white cap and khaki shirt, serves at table and performs other duties, without the mistress of the house having the slightest idea that her *servant* also serves her husband.

Usually the white man, the *msungu,* if he has no opportunity, as in Nairobi, of visiting a brothel, has his boy provide a woman for him, who, as a rule, brings him one of his discarded sweethearts, a negro prostitute who has served her duty, or his sister, who most probably sleeps for the first time with a white man, and so is very modest but complying. The first transgression of love that she committed was done some time ago; but that was with an Indian and not with a *msungu.* Almost all prostitutes have gone through his hands: the Indian is the cock in the basket. It was he who discovered her when she came into his store to buy glass beads or *merikano,* a piece of white cotton cloth. He cut off a little more for her than she had ordered, or lets the price down a bit, and manages to meet her that afternoon in the forest. For this he pays her a shilling, if he did not give her what she bought for nothing.

That was then. Now she sleeps with the *msungu* and receives five shillings or even more for the night. The master arranges another meeting with her, but does not make a definite date; he promises to have her called. There is a great demand for blacks and the *material* is scarce, and it may thus happen that she is taken for that evening, and he must therefore be without her. And on the moment the boy cannot get him another woman for the night in the God forsaken jungle, so that the master, already aroused, begins to rage. Jealousy of the woman he hates takes possession of him and changes his emotions: he all at once becomes the prey of his desire for her. He decides, perhaps with the advice of his boy, to hire her on his place for a month. That comes out cheaper anyway, because in the beginning she receives only the monthly wage, an English pound; after several months, when his concubine has quite ensnared him she is capable of getting anything she wants out of him. The whole day long she lives hidden in one of the huts of his boys, in the evening she lives in her master's soft bed, even when, in the neighboring room, he is spending half the night with his comrades drinking whiskey. A boy must bring her a wash-basin of warm water before she goes to sleep. In it, according to the rite of the Old Testament, she washes her feet that are dirty with mud. Then she lies down in the bed and soon falls asleep under the mosquito-net, that covers every thing like a canopy until her master wakes

her up. She is true to her master in so far as during all
this time she has not been making up to any white man,
nor does she like to do it even with the consent of her
master, but infidelity with the boy is no transgression to
her. Who knows how often she gives herself to the boy
out of pure joy of leading her *msungu* about by the nose!
In the course of time, such little skrimishes often turn
into fervent relationships, just like ours in Europe. The
white man is not niggardly any more, he gives her clothes,
often lets her live with him, gives her better food than
before, and does not treat her like a whore. And he receives the benefits of all this. She loves him sincerely, is
absolutely devoted to him, often keeps watch at his sick
bed with the self-sacrifice of a Samaritan: she guards him
as a dog guards his master.

The black woman is truly capable of loving a white
man. Even scenes of jealousy take place, in which, to be
sure, she does not weep, but retains her modest behavior,
whenever she sees him casting eyes on other blacks. She
may even leave him for this reason. He may go after as
many white women as he likes, that does not affect her;
but after no black without her consent. In respect to
white women she says: why, they belong to him. In
Uganda, a black woman, when she learned that her master,
a major, had taken another black, and rejected her, killed
herself, out of longing for him, by stabbing herself in the
breast. I myself read a fervent love-letter of a married
Budama woman to a young Italian, which, in spite of its
comical, broken Kisuaheli, affected us very deeply, because there we found the same human, all too human,
emotions that we had *a priori* denied to them.

The black woman is particularly respectful of the white

lady. She fears her for a reason that is believed by all blacks and which has actually become an obsession with them: the white woman, *mamzabu*, would immediately upon learning of her husband's transgression, shoot his black sweetheart with a pistol. This idea could not simply have arisen from stories which the white man incidentally tells in describing European customs. There must be some fact beneath it.

An Englishman, this was the story told me by an intelligent Nandi woman, had a black mistress. One day his wife told him that she was going to Eldoret for a few days. The man, who had not the slightest idea that his wife was only setting a trap for him, had his sweetheart come, first getting himself dead drunk with whiskey. When his wife returned the very same night, and saw the love-affair through the window, she shot the black woman. Then she carried the body away. But he, in his inebriation, slept on. When he awoke and did not find the negress beside him but instead a letter from his wife, who had gone away the very same morning, he went into the forest, found the dead woman, and shot himself beside her. All his boys had run away in fear of their mistress.

It is true that the white woman hates the black woman more than the white man hates the black man. It is no social or racial question that brings about this unchristian feeling in her. Here the struggle is a sexual one: for life and death. She sees a rival in the black woman, she sees and experiences how the white man seeks and finds in the black woman, what she had thought she alone could give him: in her, that *dirty, stinking, infected creature;* now set on an equal plane with her. I have spoken with ladies on this subject. One of them, a faded rose, divorced from her husband on account of a black, probably, asked me my opinion on whether a negress could love intensely. I answered, "Absolutely! But, naturally, to be judged by the individual case." She became pale with jealousy, her eyes moistened. Another answered my question as to what she really had against negresses, with no other objection than that they were dirty. Fundamentally, here as there, be it again emphasized, it is none other than a question of rivalry, inferiority, jealousy.

Because of the false conception of blacks that the whites have, it is really no wonder that the white man, especially the Englishman, keeps everything about the negress secret, and has consequently entirely rejected the word *black love*. He will converse on everything, especially on the prices of coffee, corn and wheat, also on the thefts that have been committed by the blacks, the way in which he had given the negro a bloody chin with his fist, or how many *kiboko* stripes he had given him. But the negress— here he breaks off the conversation. This hypocrite, this champion of mendacity, who now acts so indignant, if you ask him about a black woman . . . a black woman is already lying in his bed.

There are many tribes who have a kind of sexual aversion to white people. It is thus not so easy for a white man to get a Kavirondo woman. The reason that she does not give herself to him is, besides her great moral feeling, a superstitious one, in which her husband supports her, that the white man has a bloody member, and so all her future children would die.

If a white man seduces the wife of his boy without the latter's knowledge, murder may follow. Inflamed by thirst for revenge, he balks at no deed. The *msungu* must

246

rest content if the fellow is satisfied with setting fire to his house over his head at night. (Such a case is known to me.)

Another time, on the estate of Mr. K_____, for a similar reason, a raving servant, his best boy, in the absence of his master, took his gun, shot down many of the cattle, imprisoned and threatened the son of the house causing his mother to run to his aid and thus was able to rape her. He was finally overpowered. For mitigating reasons he was only imprisoned for five years. When he left the jail he was supposed to have said that the first thing he would do, would be: to kill his master.

The love of a white man for a black woman has as yet not gone so far as to necessitate sealing it with marriage. Even the missionary, who always keeps talking of loving one's neighbors, has not succeeded in crossing the Chinese wall of classes, race aversions, and race hatred. With one exception, however, but which remained an unsuccessful attempt.

In Nyangori, the American missionary, Mr. M. had actually carried the teaching of Christ into practice. He loved the blacks like his own countrymen, ate and slept with them in his house, which fact alone bred ill blood among the white population. But public opinion did not become hot until he tried to marry a black woman. He had already given the parents of his bride the necessary dowry, and the marriage day had been set. But his white brothers succeeded, through pressure, in making the girl's father give his little daughter to the sultan of the village to add to his harem. But the cup of the shepherd of the people was not yet full. During the devotional exercise in the church, he had to stand insults from the black flock, instigated by the whites. Quite broken, he left his thankless flock and returned to America. The curse of class and race broke two souls.

The problem of race mixture, not to say that of race deterioration, is not so acute in East Africa as in other places. While the population of South Africa, and of the various African islands (the Seychelles, where the black population of the country speaks only French, St. Helena, etc.), as in South America, consists, to a great extent of bastards between whites and non-whites. In East Africa, hybrid blood is practically unseen, because, strangely enough, these mixed marriages here seldom result in children. For example, the Nandi woman, in her relations with whites, is, for some reason unknown to me, usually sterile. Hybrids are therefore seldom met with. A thirteen year old girl, the daughter of a government official and a Nandi woman, already married, attracted not so much by her somewhat lighter, fine, copper-red color, and slighter build, but rather by the different growth of her hair, which was not woolly, but smooth like that of a European woman. She was about to be circumcised, and did not look any different than her playmates, except in what has been mentioned, but her eyes seemed to me to be that of an English girl.

In Uganda I saw a suckling, a hybrid between a Mnioro girl and an Italian, that looked quite like an Arab child. The eyes of hybrids suffer, especially in the piercing rays of the tropic sun, apparently because they are not inherently accustomed to being carried around naked and bare-headed, like the less sensitive natives.

It hurts one, meeting such children. As a rule their fathers do not bother about them in the least, so that they